Painting & Wallpapering

Created and Designed by the Editorial Staff of Ortho Books

Project Editors
Robert J. Beckstrom
Sally W. Smith

Writer
Sharon Ross

Technical Consultant
Brian Santos

Ortho Books

Publisher
Robert B. Loperena

Editorial Director
Christine Jordan

Manufacturing Director
Ernie S. Tasaki

Managing Editor
Sally W. Smith

Editor
Robert J. Beckstrom

Prepress Supervisor
Linda M. Bouchard

Editorial Assistants
Joni Christiansen
Sally J. French

Address all inquiries to:
Ortho Books
Box 5006
San Ramon, CA 94583-0906

Copyright © 1983, 1995
Monsanto Company
All rights reserved under international and Pan-American copyright conventions.

1 2 3 4 5 6 7 8 9
95 96 97 98 99 2000

ISBN 0-89721-259-2
Library of Congress Catalog Card Number 94-69599

THE SOLARIS GROUP
2527 Camino Ramon
San Ramon, CA 94583-0906

Illustrators
Mark Egge, Brian Jensen, and
  Leslie Jensen, RKB Studios

Editorial Coordinator
Cass Dempsey

Copyeditor
Toni Murray

Proofreader
Alicia K. Eckley

Indexer
Elinor Lindheimer

Separations by
Color Tech Corp.

Lithographed in the USA by
Banta Company

Special Thanks to
Benjamin Moore & Company
Centers for Disease Control,
  U.S. Department of Health
  and Human Services
Deborah Cowder
Hirschfield's
Imperial Wallcoverings
Knox Lumber, Payless
  Cashways
National Decorating Products
  Association
National Paint and Coating
  Association
Norton Abrasive Coatings
  Company
Painting and Decorating
  Contractors of America
Rohm and Haas Paint Quality
  Institute
The Color Association of the
  United States
The Glidden Company
The Sherwin-Williams
  Company
The Wallcovering Information
  Bureau
3M
Valspar
David Van Ness
Wagner Spray Tech Company
Carol Waldron
Wallcoverings Association
Wallcovering Industry Council
William A. Zinzer Company

Photographers
Names of photographers are followed by the page numbers on which their work appears.
David Livingston: 1, 4–5, 9BR, 10T, 10B, 12T, 12BR, 17, 19, 20–21, 37B, 55, 56B, 57L, 57R, 69TL, 69BL
Stephen Marley: 16B
Geoffrey Nilsen: 14T, 14BL, 14BR, 23, 24T, 24B, 27, 37T, 42, 53T, 53BL, 53BR, 54T, 54BL, 54BR, 58, 60, 61, 62, 72; front cover, small photographs; back cover
Kenneth Rice: 9T, 9BL, 11, 12BL, 13, 16T, 18B, 34–35, 56T, 89
Jessie Walker Associates: 18T, 64–65, 67TL, 67TR, 67BL, 67BR, 69TR, 69BR, 77, 84; front cover, large photograph

Architects, Designers, and Builders
Names of architects, designers, and builders are followed by the page numbers on which their work appears.
Richard Banks: 1, 37B
Lou Ann Bauer: 9BR, 12BR
The Beardsley Co.: 11
Diane Chapman: 10T, 17, 20–21, 55, 57R
Melissa Charles and Susan Kline, Montclair Children's Shop: 89
Cole-Wheatman, Inc.: 16B
Marjorie Davis: 69TR
Roger Dobbel: 10B
Judy Dodd Interiors: 4–5
Robert Feigal: 69BL
Gwynn-Hogland Interior Design: 18B
Barbara Hutchings: 57L
Glen Jarvis and Steve Smith Construction: 16T
Robert Korach: 18T
Carol Knott, A.S.I.D.: 64–65, 67TR, 69BR
David Livingston Interiors: 56B
Alexandra Owen: 9T
Alice Paul: 19
Robert Pitt: 67BL
Barbara Scavullo and Arnelle Kase, Barbara Scavullo Design: 34–35
Carol Shawn: 12T
Jula Sutta Design Associates: 12BL
Tedrick & Bennett: 13
Linda Thomas, A.S.I.D.: front cover
Stella Tuttle: 69TL
Wasson II: 9BL

Front Cover
Left, top to bottom: Only a few, simple techniques are required to apply paint quickly and evenly with a roller.

Stenciling is an effective and easy way to create hand-painted borders in virtually any design imaginable.

To make a smooth surface, "float" the wall by applying joint compound in two thin layers with a wide taping knife.
Top center: Two secrets to seamless patching are providing a stable base for the compound—such as the fiberglass mesh shown here—and appling the compound in several stages.
Top right: Dragging is one of many decorative effects that can be created with paint and a few simple tools. Here, a dry brush is dragged over fresh paint applied with a roller.
Bottom right: Bold, lively, and fresh, this floral wallcovering is coordinated with the bedspread and window coverings for a cheerful effect.

Title Page
Created by subtle glazes and ragging, the decorative paint technique used on these plaster walls adds richness, depth, and texture to the neutral colors.

Page 3
Top: The intricate color scheme of this room is built around a set of logical relationships, starting with the lemon-yellow and ice-blue stripes painted on the walls. Blue and yellow are primary colors that, when combined, create green—which is used in the room's fabrics. The third primary color, red, a complement of green, appears as an accent color.
Bottom: Rolling a rag over fresh paint creates a textured effect similar to rich leather or aged plaster walls.

Back Cover
These four sample boards were primed identically and painted with latex paints of the same off-white color—only the sheens are different. The upper-left board is painted with high gloss paint, the upper right is eggshell, the lower right is semigloss, and the lower left is flat.

Painting & Wallpapering

DECORATING WITH COLOR, TEXTURE & PATTERN

You are about to embark on a decorating adventure. No one denies that painting and wallcovering are messy and time-consuming, but they are also rewarding. They give you the satisfaction of doing something creative with your hands and the pleasure of watching a new, colorful surface emerge beneath your fingers. Most important of all, they give you the tools—color, texture, and pattern—for covering the large surfaces that form the background of a room's decorating scheme. Therein lies the adventure. These tools become the keys to the magic world of decorating. This chapter introduces you to the pleasures of working with color, texture, and pattern. You will learn techniques for creating your own color scheme, and the way to apply those techniques in choosing paints and wallcoverings. The remaining three chapters show you how to apply those versatile products to any wall or ceiling, with professional-looking results.

Walls don't have to be quiet. The intense color and sumptuous texture of these painted walls make them a dominant, but not overwhelming, element in this handsome room.

REFINING YOUR COLOR SENSE

Color is magic. It has such impact that it produces emotional and physical responses. It is so versatile that it can be divided into countless tints, shades, and tones. These qualities make the use of color subjective and highly personal. There are no absolutes, no rigid rules. But there are principles that govern how colors work together.

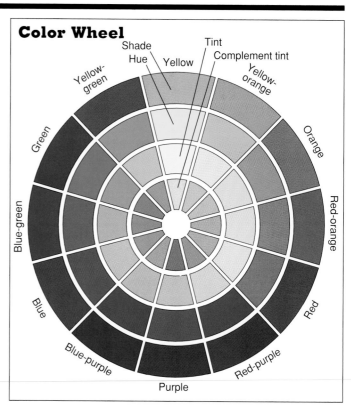

Color Wheel

Understanding Color Basics

Effective design begins with color. It can set a room's personality, define its style, control its mood, alter its space, accent its advantages, hide its faults, and turn an otherwise dull space into something wonderful and inviting. The problem is, one color alone won't do these things, because no color can exist on its own in decorating. It needs other colors to reinforce or modify it. That is why you need to develop pleasing color combinations when you decorate a room. To do this effectively, you must know two things: how colors relate to and influence one another, and how to use contrast to control these interactions. Learn to manipulate color this way and you can build color schemes that make rooms lively, interesting, and harmonious. This ability to control color—what designers call a color sense—is based on a series of principles that you can learn.

The first principle is that color has three dimensions: hue, value, and intensity. The way they are combined gives each color its unique identity. Hue is the basic ingredient. It's easy to understand because hues can be organized into a simple system of relationships that is known as the color wheel.

Hue and the Color Wheel

Hue is the aspect of color we are most familiar with. The term *hue,* in fact, can be considered another word for *color.* Red, blue, and green are hues. So are amber, teal, lilac, and taupe. The color wheel shows the relationships among the various colors. These relationships, in turn, are the basis for building attractive color schemes for your home. If you've wondered why some colors work together and others don't, the answer is not whim; it's science—the physics of light. In simple terms, when you see color, you really see light reflected by an object. Light travels in waves from its source, to an object, to your eyes. These light waves have different lengths, and each wavelength creates a specific color image. Thus, which color you see depends on the number and length of the light waves reflected off an object.

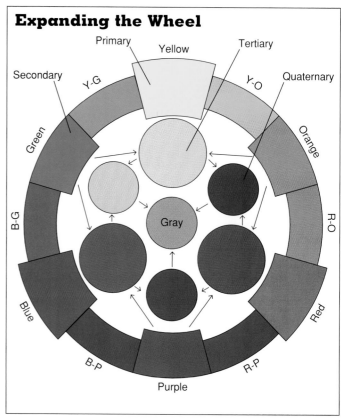

Expanding the Wheel

The Language of Color

Advancing colors The warm colors. Like dark colors, they seem to make surfaces move toward the eye.

Analogous colors Any three colors located next to one another on the color wheel.

Color scheme A group of colors used together to create visual unity in a room.

Color wheel A circular arrangement of the 12 basic colors that shows how they relate to one another. It includes the three primary colors—red, yellow, and blue—the three secondary colors, and the six intermediate colors. The color wheel was developed by Sir Isaac Newton after studying the effects of passing a beam of light through a prism.

Complementary colors Colors located opposite one another on the color wheel.

Cool colors The blues, greens, and purples.

Contrast The principle of assembling colors with different values and intensities to create a color scheme.

Hue Synonym for color.

Intensity The brightness or dullness of a color. Also referred to as the purity or saturation of a color.

Intermediate colors The six colors made by mixing equal amounts of a primary and a secondary color. They are red-orange, yellow-orange, yellow-green, blue-green, blue-purple and red-purple.

Primary colors The pure colors—red, yellow, and blue—that cannot be broken down into other colors. They are the basis for all other colors.

Quaternary colors Colors made by mixing together equal amounts of two tertiary colors.

Receding colors The cool colors. Like light colors, they seem to make surfaces move away from the eye.

Secondary colors Orange, green, and purple—the colors created by mixing equal amounts of two primary colors.

Shade A color to which black has been added to make it darker.

Split complementary A color combination that consists of a color joined with the colors on either side of its complement.

Tertiary colors Colors made by mixing equal amounts of two secondary colors.

Tint A color to which white has been added to make it lighter. Also called a pastel.

Tone A color modified with gray.

Triad A color combination consisting of any three colors located equidistant from one another on the color wheel.

Value The lightness or darkness of a color.

Value scale A tool used to show the range of values between pure white and pure black.

Visible spectrum The bands of colors created when light is passed through a prism.

Warm colors The reds, oranges, and yellows, including the browns.

White contains all these wavelengths in the same proportion as they occur in sunlight. As sunlight passes through a prism, the wavelengths bend at different angles and break into a beautiful spectrum, or rainbow. It seems to have six colors (three primary and three secondary): purple (the shortest wavelength), blue, green, yellow, orange, and red (the longest wavelength), in that order. If you look closely, you will see these colors blending to form six more. Organizing the spectrum into a circular format, or color wheel, makes it possible to see clear relationships among these 12 colors.

The Primary Colors

The three pure colors found in light—red, yellow, and blue—are called primary colors because they cannot be broken down into other colors and because they are used to create all others. They lie equal distances apart on the color wheel.

The Secondary Colors

These are orange, green, and purple. Each is created from equal amounts of two primary colors: red and yellow make orange; yellow and blue make green; and blue and red create purple. On the color wheel, each secondary color falls halfway between the two primary colors it contains, and directly opposite the third.

The Intermediate Colors

Bridging the spaces between the primary and secondary colors are the intermediate colors—red-orange, yellow-orange, yellow-green, blue-green, blue-purple, and red-purple. They contain equal amounts of a primary and a secondary color. Thus, red (a primary) and orange (a secondary) combine to make red-orange (an intermediate).

Tertiary and Quaternary Colors

The potential for color variations increases when you combine two secondary colors to create a tertiary color. Purple and orange, for example, create a reddish brown with purple undertones that could be called terra-cotta. Combine two tertiary colors and you make a quaternary color. The resulting colors are richer than the pure hues. These third- and fourth-tier colors do not appear on the typical color wheel and are difficult to describe because they are such complex blends. That is why they are often given names drawn from nature, geography, and history rather than standard color names.

The Neutral Colors

These are white; black; and all grays, which are blends of white and black. Theoretically, white and black are noncolors because they either reflect all the colors in the visible spectrum (white) or absorb all of them (black). These neutral colors do not appear on the color wheel.

Opposite Colors Attract

The color wheel illustrates more than how colors evolve from one another. It also helps you determine which colors will work well together. There are no hard-and-fast rules about which colors should be used together, but there are natural combinations that are always successful. The list that follows describes the most common pairings.

•Complementary colors: Colors located across the color wheel from one another. Yellow and purple are complements. So are red-orange and blue-green. Complements stimulate one another, but can seem garish if used together full strength. If paints of complementary colors are literally mixed together in equal amounts, they neutralize one another and produce a flat, dull gray color.

•Analogous colors: Three colors that occur beside one another on the color wheel.

•Triad colors: Three equidistant colors. Red, blue, and yellow are a triad.

•Split complementary: A color plus the color on each side of its complement. Pairing red with blue-green and yellow-green makes a split complementary scheme.

•Double split complementary: Four colors, one from each side of two complementary colors. This is a very rich color scheme, but difficult to do well.

Value and Intensity

Pure colors are seldom used in interior design. Instead, they are altered to increase their subtlety and soften their impact. Such adjustments, called extending the color range, are made by mixing the 12 basic colors with one another or with white, black, or gray, in different proportions. The result is colors that vary from the pure hues in value and intensity, which makes them more pleasing and interesting. (The number of variations is endless, which is fortunate because the human eye can distinguish 10 million different colors.) Value and intensity control the contrast between colors. That contrast is the essential ingredient in a successful color scheme.

Color Value

Value refers to the lightness or darkness of a hue. As a color is mixed with white, gray, or black, it moves away from its pure hue, becoming a tint or a shade. A tint is a hue that has been lightened by adding white to it. The more white, the paler the color. For example, pinks are tints of red. A shade is a color that has been darkened by adding black to it. The more black, the darker the color. Forest green is a shade of green. A tone is a color that has been modified with gray. Mustard is a tone of yellow. On the color wheel, tints lie

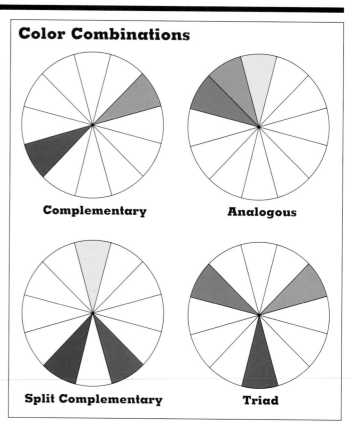

Color Combinations

Complementary **Analogous**

Split Complementary **Triad**

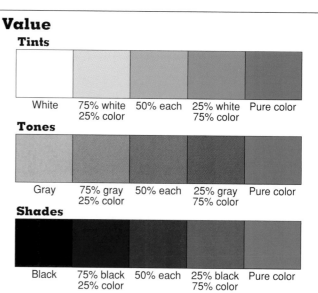

Value

Tints

| White | 75% white 25% color | 50% each | 25% white 75% color | Pure color |

Tones

| Gray | 75% gray 25% color | 50% each | 25% gray 75% color | Pure color |

Shades

| Black | 75% black 25% color | 50% each | 25% black 75% color | Pure color |

inside the pure hues and move toward the center as they get progressively lighter. Shades lie outside the pure hues and move outward as they get darker. Tones generally do not appear on the color wheel.

The color value of a specific hue can be judged against a value scale. This is a vertical bar divided into 10 sections, ranging from pure white at the top to black at the bottom. In between are grays that

become progressively darker in 10-percent increments. All the colors at the same level on the bar have the same value. One method of controlling the contrast between different colors is by using them in different values. Blue and green, for instance, don't always work well together, but a pastel blue and a dark green can be a very pleasing combination.

Color Intensity

Intensity, or *chroma*, describes a color's degree of purity, or saturation. This can be a difficult concept; think of intensity as describing a color's brightness or dullness undiluted by tinting or shading. A color can be dark and bright or light and dull—the nuances of color are wonderful. You increase a color's intensity by adding more of the pure hue. The more hue, the more vivid and intense the color appears to the eye. You reduce its intensity by adding either black or its complementary color to it. The more you add, the grayer and duller the color becomes. To create more contrasts between colors, add intensity to the mix of values and hues in the color scheme. As an example, khaki, a low-intensity color, contrasts nicely with royal blue, an intense color.

Warm and Cool Colors

Colors have one more dimension that should be considered: their visual temperature. Colors are either warm or cool, a quality related to their ability to influence people,

Varying the values and intensities of the three primary colors (top), and combining subtly different blues and greens (bottom), transform pure hues into refined blends of color.

The strong warm tones of these two rooms are calmed and cooled by neutrals and greens.

Color's Emotional Impact

Color is often used to describe emotions: red with anger, green with envy, sad to the point of being blue, rosy with optimism. There's even purple passion. Colors do stimulate emotional and physical reactions in people. Each color has a psychological value that must be considered when selecting a color for a room, so the color feels right as well as looks right.

Red

Red is a warm, bold, stirring, and energetic color. In its pure form it can increase heart rate and raise body temperature. Associated with royal pomp as well as favorite flowers and fruits, red is a color of strong and sometimes contradictory contrasts. Pink, a tint, suggests feminine charms; pure red is the color for military courage and stop signs. Vibrant and passionate, red is enjoyed by everyone, especially children, but it is seldom used in its pure hue on large surfaces, such as walls, because it is so powerful.

Yellow and Orange

Yellow and orange are just as exciting as red, but they are more cheerful than festive, more bright than stimulating. They are associated with the color of the sun and the warmth of fire. Yellow and orange warm and enliven any room in which they are used. They exist in many variations, from the bright yellow of daisies to the deep yellow of fall mums, from the color

of peaches and apricots to the color of autumn leaves. All of them speak of things glowing with life, which makes these hues excellent to use where food is served or where you want people to be outgoing and happy. On large surfaces, they are best used in light values.

Green

Green is the dominant color in nature. As such, it is a pleasing, cool, fresh, calming, even restful color, and it produces these reactions in people. It is the color of nature's bounty, so it can be seen as natural and alive. It ranges from the pale yellow-green of a key lime to the deep green of wine bottles to the cool blue-greens, such as turquoise, which are more green than blue. It is a color for any room where you want a calm, relaxed, but fresh atmosphere.

Blue

Blue, the color of sky and water, creates images of freshness, coolness, and restfulness. Blue walls can make a south- or west-facing room feel cooler. Because it "recedes," blue also creates the illusion of space and distance, conjuring up emotions of haughtiness, formality, reserve, and sadness. In spite of evoking such contradictory reactions, blue is a favorite because it is so easy on the eyes and the nerves. This ease makes it an excellent choice for rooms where you want to relax, even sleep. Blue ranges from the teals and aquas (blue-green colors that are

more blue than green) through the blue-purples.

Purple

Purple calls up images of lushness, regality, and passion. It is an intense and highly emotional color, partly because it straddles the line between the warm and cool colors. This makes it a difficult color to use in interior design, and it is usually confined to the role of an accent.

However, tints and shade of its analogous hues, blue-purple and red-purple, are very attractive and add liveliness to any interior.

Black and White

Black and white are pure contrasts, light and nonlight. That is what makes them so sophisticated. Both dramatic and elegant, they conjure up stylish images.

physically or psychologically. Any color that has yellow or red in it is a warm color. As such it is stimulating and inviting. Scientific tests have shown that a room painted a warm color will feel warmer than a room painted white or a cool color, even though they are at the same temperature. Warm colors "advance" toward you because their long light waves make them seem nearer than they are. That's why they make a room shrink visually.

A cool color is any color that has blue in it, plus the neutral colors white, gray, and black. Cool colors are fresh, calm, comfortable, and non-confining. Those same color tests have shown that, on a hot afternoon, a west-facing room painted blue or gray will feel cooler than a room painted a warm color, even though the temperature of both rooms is the same. Cool colors "recede" because their shorter light waves make them seem farther away. That is why they work so well in small rooms.

Sources of Color Inspiration

Good designers have an eye for color, an eye trained to recognize the variety of colors available and how they work together. *Trained* is the key word here. Designers learn this skill, they are not born with it. You can develop the same skilled eye by studying how color around you is used. Here are some ideas.

•Start with nature, from the brilliant plumage of birds to the dramatic colors of a seashore sunset. Nature doesn't make mistakes.

•Look at paintings and tapestries in museums and art books. All artwork is an excellent source of inspiration, but the works of the Impressionists are especially helpful because they show how colors placed side by side merge visually to create another color when viewed from a distance.

•Study decorative fabrics, from oriental rugs to drapery and upholstery fabrics.

•Read decorating magazines. The articles are excellent resources because the homes they discuss are created by top interior designers.

•Study fine-quality wallcoverings. Books of such wallcoverings are available at wallcovering dealers, and you can take them home.

•Browse the showrooms in high-quality furniture stores. The displays, arranged by trained interior designers, emphasize effective color schemes in order to sell the store's total design services. A similar source of ideas is model homes and decorator showcases. Look at the specific hues, values, and intensities used, and the proportions between them. Try to relate what you see to the color wheel, and note those combinations you find particularly pleasing.

A word of caution: Beware of color trends. Such trends arise from manufacturers trying to keep ahead of public taste. Color forecasters predict what the new colors will be. Manufacturers begin making everything from bath towels to picture frames in these new

hues, and soon it becomes difficult to find affordable merchandise in other colors. Suddenly, what seemed new and exciting becomes so common it grows old, and the manufacturers start looking for new colors. To protect yourself, use the colors that please you, whether or not they are in style. Combine them in effective color schemes and you won't have to worry about your home looking dated.

Enriching Color With Texture

Color may be the most powerful decorating element, but it is influenced and refined in

subtle ways by texture and pattern. Learning how to use these two elements gives you more tools for working with color. They are particularly pertinent to wallcoverings, although texture also plays a role in working with paints.

Texture is the surface quality of a material—how it looks to the eye (visual texture) and feels to the hand (tactile texture). Usually, it comes into a room via fabrics and carpeting, although not always. All paint and wallcoverings have visual texture and sometimes tactile texture. Either way, texture is as emotionally pleasing as color, and influences it as surely as colors influence one another.

Like color, texture is multidimensional. It can range from

This subtle, delicate color scheme might have been inspired by the prints, the flowers, or even towels on display in a store.

rough to smooth, hard to soft, and shiny to dull. You can put these dimensions together in many combinations to express any mood or style you desire. For example, a wallcovering or decorative paint technique can use layers of colors to create the effect of a rough surface. That is what the eye sees, but the hand feels something that is smooth. However texture is used, it adds visual spice to a room.

Texture and Paint

A paint's texture is created by its degree of surface reflection. This can range from the light-absorbing finish of a flat paint to the light-reflecting luster of a high-gloss paint. The first produces colors that appear subdued and darker than they

are. The second makes colors appear brighter and lighter than they are. Each also creates a distinct environment. The flat finish, whether used in a formal or informal setting, is understated; the high-gloss finish is sophisticated. A texture ingredient can be added to paint to produce a coarse surface when desired. In addition, paint can be applied in decorative finishes—such as sponging, stippling, and ragging—to add visual depth and character to color.

Texture and Wallcoverings

All wallcoverings have more visual texture than paint because their patterns create the feeling of an uneven surface even if they are smooth to

From smooth and glossy to luxuriously soft, the interplay of textures in these three rooms complements the rich blends of color. Notice how various sheens of wall paint add to the visual texture.

the touch. Some wallcoverings—such as burlap, grass cloth, string cloth, linen weaves, suedes, flocks, moirés, and relief papers—also have tactile texture and are truly three-dimensional. They become a dominant element in any room in which they are used.

Enriching Color With Pattern

Pattern is the two-dimensional decorative design on a wallcovering. It is as important as color. For instance, a well-designed pattern can effectively juxtapose so many colors that it opens up the range of hues available for use in a color scheme. A well-chosen design

will enhance a room's colors. That's why thoughtful contrasts in pattern can enrich the overall visual effect of a room.

The Basics of Pattern

Pattern adds interest to a room's overall design and interacts with its decorative style. A properly chosen pattern unifies a room's color scheme and textures. Most important of all, it emphasizes lines, shape, and architectural features. That is why the pattern must suit the size and shape of a room as much as the decorative style. To use pattern successfully, break a pattern down into its elements and then assess them in relationship to the room.

Motifs

Wallcovering patterns fall into seven motif categories.

•Large prints: Most often realistic or stylized designs of natural forms such as flowers. Colorful and dominant. Best suited to large spaces.

•Small prints: Like large prints, only smaller. Also softer and less dominant. Work well in medium-sized and small rooms.

•Mini prints: Tiny motifs scattered across the surface. Work well in small spaces and as contrasts to bold companion prints.

•Geometrics: Designs made up of stripes, checks, plaids, and other geometric shapes. Have a decidedly contemporary feel.

•Abstract: Loose designs that use color to give the illusion of shapes or the impression of depth. Very contemporary in feeling.

•Textures: Designs that are truly three-dimensional, like fabrics or plasterwork.

•Borders: Designed to coordinate with any of the motifs, borders can also be used alone.

Within each motif category you will find specific patterns suitable to each decorating style. Decide which category and decorating style you want before you begin your search. This will dramatically narrow your choices and make your selection job much easier.

How to Work With a Professional Interior Designer

If color intimidates you, or your decorating situation is particularly complex, or you would just like a little personal guidance, consider hiring a professional interior designer as a consultant. Many professionals work on an hourly basis. They can help you define your style, interpret your needs, and choose the right colors, textures, and patterns for your project. They can also help you with attractive, workable room arrangements and provide access to decorating materials that are available only to professionals. These items—which are labeled "to the trade only" and which include all types of decorative fabrics, wallcoverings, carpets, furniture,

and accessories—are not sold at retail. A pro's fees can range from $25 to $125 per hour or more, so ask up front what a consultation will cost and specify the exact number of hours of service you want. Even one hour of time can be of great benefit. You will consider it money well spent if it helps you avoid a costly mistake or a major disappointment. To locate a designer near you, ask for recommendations from friends, look under "Interior Decorators & Designers" in the yellow pages, or ask for a referral from a professional interior design organization such as the American Society of Interior Designers, in Washington, D.C. (202-546-3480).

This room might have been overwhelmed by the boldly patterned fabric, but muted colors, flowing fabrics, and gracefully curved furniture keep the checks in check.

The same room with three different wallcoverings—only the scale of the patterns varies. A large pattern (top left) pulls the wall inward and makes the room feel smaller; a small pattern (bottom) seems to enlarge the space.

Design Dimensions

Pattern has three dimensions: scale, line, and rhythm.

•Scale: This is the size of the design in relationship to the room and its furnishings. You want to balance the two so you neither overwhelm nor underplay a room. In a large room, a large floral print will emphasize its generous space and create a sense of formality. It can actually make an oversized room seem more human in scale because it will pull the walls closer. However, a mini print will get lost in a large room—unless you simply want it to create a feeling of texture, not pattern.

•Line: Most patterns have line, a dominant vertical or horizontal feeling. This is especially true of the geometric and abstract patterns, many mini prints, and the small prints, such as those with ribbons. Line should enhance a room's size and shape. For example, if a room is long and narrow or has a high ceiling, don't use a wall-covering with a strong vertical line; visually, it will make the room seem even higher and narrower. However, if the ceiling is low, that vertical push would make the space seem more comfortable. Random, overall patterns work best in most rooms, unless the room is so angular that the pattern will be broken up too much.

•Rhythm: The repetition of motifs creates rhythm, the sense of unity you feel as your eyes move over the pattern. Rhythm, in turn, creates a sense of harmony within a room. If the room is to be a place to rest and relax, you want a pattern with a quiet or subdued rhythm. However, if it is to be a place of activity, it should have a vigorous rhythm.

DEVELOPING A COLOR SCHEME

It's time to take what you've learned about color, texture, and pattern, and build a color scheme for your room. Paint and wallcoverings will play a major role in this scheme, but you must take into account all the features and furnishings of the room, from carpet to artwork. Here are some guidelines to help you.

Getting Started

Walls are the biggest surfaces in most rooms. How you finish them affects everything else you do in that space, but that doesn't mean they have to dominate it. You control the dominant effect by deciding, in the beginning, whether the walls will be the room's backdrop or its focal point.

Background Walls

If walls are to be the backdrop, choose their color after selecting the other major elements. Then you can pull a coordinating color from one of those sources. This color can be a shade or tint of the dominant color; a shade or tint pulled from a pattern used in the room, whether in the carpet, decorative fabrics, or wallcovering; or a shade or tint drawn from a painting, an important piece of furniture, a fireplace surround, or even the view. It also can be a shade or tint of a color complementary to the dominant color. You probably will find that complement used in one of the patterned fabrics in the room. This is the

way to choose a new finish for the walls in a room where nothing else will be changed.

An alternate choice is to use a neutral color on the walls. That makes them a true backdrop because the walls will not call attention to themselves. This is a time-proven and safe solution; it is why the majority of walls are still painted white. However, be aware that white is not just white. There are more than sixty variations of whites from which you can pick, each with subtle differences in tint, value, intensity, and visual warmth. Choose carefully.

There are good reasons for selecting the wall treatment after the other elements are set. This approach lets you find the one color whose balance of hue, value, and intensity will complement all the colors in the room, in much the same way as the matting around a picture emphasizes its colors. Also, thanks to modern techniques for matching and mixing custom colors, it is easy to match a paint to the colors in a carpet or fabric. On the other hand, it is practically impossible to find a carpet or fabric that matches an existing paint color.

Focal-Point Walls

If the walls are to be the most important feature in the room as well as the largest, choose their finish first and then build your scheme around it. This is more difficult to do than picking a background color because, like an artist starting with a clean canvas, you have to decide where you are going to go without reference to anything else. There are several ways you can go about making your choice.

Identify Your Favorite Colors

Review the most pleasing colors and color combinations you found while studying color, texture, and pattern. What colors were you drawn to, time after time? What colors made you feel happy or whole? Look at your clothes. What colors dominate your wardrobe? What colors are you most often wearing when people compliment you on your appearance? These are the colors you naturally favor, and since people are happiest with the colors they like, this makes them the best colors for your home.

Study the Room's Mood

A room's environment is determined by a combination of many things, such as its function, decorative style, size, natural light, and exterior weather conditions. You must determine which of these influences is the most important in a specific room and then select a paint or wallcovering that enhances that influence. Your choices will focus mainly on whether the room should be light or dark, warm or cool. Only two, very general guidelines apply here. If a room receives minimal light, the wall color should be light—unless, of course, you want the room to be dark and cozy. Whatever wall finish is used, its color, texture, and pattern should be suitable to the room's decorative style. Beyond that, do what you want to do.

Consider Any Problems

Color, texture, and pattern have the ability to "move" walls and ceilings in relation to the viewer. In general, light colors, subtle textures, and small patterns make a room seem larger and higher, so they are ideal choices when you want the room to seem larger than it is or when you want to emphasize the spaciousness of the room. If the ceiling is too low, consider a strongly vertical pattern. Dark or intense colors; bold, coarse textures; and large or busy patterns make a room seem smaller because they bring the

Top: The gray walls of this comfortable den provide a noncompetitive background for the crisp, white woodwork and color-coordinated fabrics.
Bottom: The restrained neutral color scheme gives this room a calm, refined mood.

walls closer to you. That's desirable in a room that is too large, especially if you want a cozy, intimate effect. It's also desirable if you want to emphasize the comfortable snugness of a small room.

When it comes to woodwork or other architectural features, decide whether you want them hidden or highlighted. If you would like them to disappear, paint them a color that matches the wall, to diminish their presence; to make them stand out, paint them a contrasting hue.

Choosing Colors

An effective color scheme usually combines no more than three colors, plus a neutral. Fight the impulse to add more colors; instead, use variations in value and intensity to create contrast between colors. The color wheel (see page 6) will help you choose colors that work well together. However, the colors you are considering will seldom be the pure hues of the color wheel, so it is important to visualize where

the colors would fall on the color wheel. The four combinations listed on page 8, and two others, are considered classics. They are the easiest for beginners and those with modest experience to use.

Complementary

This scheme uses two colors that lie directly opposite one another on the color wheel. The best example is the red and green of Christmas. Another example is peach (red-orange) and turquoise

(blue-green). Because it combines exact opposites, this combination balances warm and cool colors and tends to be lively. It will also be garish unless you achieve contrast by using different values and intensities.

Analogous

This scheme blends three contiguous colors—colors lying next to one another on the color wheel. Yellow-orange, yellow, and yellow-green make an analogous arrangement. So do blue-green, blue, and blue-purple. This is a harmonious plan because the colors are closely related and your eyes pass over them with ease.

Triad

This combination puts together three colors located equal distances from one another. Red, yellow, and blue make a triad, as do blue-purple, yellow-green and red-orange. This is a complex, lively color scheme, so controlling values and intensities is important.

Split Complementary

This variation on the complementary scheme combines a color with the colors on either side of its complement. Yellow combined with red-purple and blue-purple is an example. This subtle shift in the complementary colors enriches the scheme.

A complementary color scheme, based on variations of red and green, contributes to the fresh, spirited mood of this room.

Monochromatic

Here, one color is used in many values and intensities so the mix stays lively and interesting. This is a sophisticated scheme that needs texture contrasts to work well.

Neutral

This plan uses whites, grays, and black to build an elegant color palette. Some designers include browns, from cream to chocolate, in this category. The neutral scheme needs value, intensity, and texture contrasts to be effective.

Note that, in most of these formulas, a range of values and intensities is needed to use the colors to their best advantage. For instance, in the case of the classic red and green of Christmas, the red is a pure and intense hue and the green is deeper than the pure hue, darker in value and lower in intensity.

Determining the Proportions of Colors

Mixing the best colors in the right proportion is the most important part of a color scheme. It's also the most difficult. Few people have so much skill combining colors, at least in the beginning, that they can assemble a final color scheme with the confidence and finesse of a professional designer. Most people tend to use a favorite color over and over until it loses its impact. You can avoid that mistake by following one of these tried-and-true approaches.

These two rooms both feature red, white, and blue, but in vastly different proportions and of different values.

Strong, bold colors can be successfully combined if they are wisely chosen and carefully balanced.

only two colors, you must pay special attention to the mix of contrasting values and intensities. You must also add texture contrasts to the total scheme. The textures can be in the paint or wallcovering, or in the upholstery and accessory fabrics.

Testing Your Choices

Because everything in the room will affect the color or pattern you will use, take time to make a sample board so you can test your choices on-site. Making such a board costs you a little money up front, but it will save you a costly mistake down the line. Buy a quart of the paint or a roll of the wallcovering you are considering and use it to cover a 2- by 4-foot piece of plywood. Put this board in the room and study how it appears at different times of day. Pay special attention to how it appears at the time of day you are most likely to use the room. Also, move the board around so you can see how the color and pattern choices look in different parts of the room. A color that looks wonderful on the wall opposite a window may look dreadful high up in a corner or on a wall that doesn't receive direct light. Test the board against furnishings or room features, such as floor covering or fireplace. If it turns out your choice does not work, start over with a new selection and a new sample board.

One Color Dominant

Use one color in its different values and intensities over most of the room, then use its complementary, analogous, triad, or split-complementary colors as accents on smaller furniture pieces, window coverings, accent rugs, and accessories such as pillows.

A monochromatic arrangement is another version of this design plan. It also uses one color in shades and tints of different values. However, only one accent color is used. It is a contrast of the base color, often its complement.

Split Colors

Use one color on the walls, the window coverings, and most upholstered furniture. Use a different color on the floor, and a third color and variations of the first two for the pieces of accent furniture and accessories. This is an excellent way to use a triad or split-complementary color combination. Just be sure you get significant contrast in the colors' values and intensities.

Two Dominant Colors

Here you use one dominant color for the walls, floor, and smaller pieces of furniture, and another color for the major pieces of furniture. Because you are working with

PREPARATION

Whether you are painting or papering, the most important step in the process is preparation. All room surfaces should be prepped—repaired, smoothed, and scrubbed—before they are refinished. You may be tempted to skip these tedious tasks. Don't. Many people mistakenly assume that a coat of fresh paint or a layer of new wallcovering will hide surface defects. They won't. They will actually magnify the faults. That's why professional painters allow one to three hours of prep time for every hour they will spend painting or papering. You should do the same. This chapter presents prep techniques for any kind of surface to be refinished. The techniques you use depend on the type of surface you plan to refinish and whether you will paint or paper it. Last but not least, preparation should always include a review of safety tips to observe throughout your project.

Wood-paneled walls offer exciting possibilities for paint. Careful preparation, to eliminate flaws and ensure proper paint adhesion, makes it possible to dress up the most rustic den with graceful lines and textures.

SETTING UP FOR THE JOB

Scraping paint, stripping wallpaper, applying wallboard compound, sanding rough surfaces, and scrubbing walls are messy jobs. They will be easier and will go more quickly if you first take time to prepare the room, procure the right tools and materials, and review all safety procedures.

Pickup and Cleanup

The painter's (or wallcoverer's) dream room is an empty room. Remove as much of the furniture as possible. Place pieces that can't be removed in the center of the room and cover them, first with plastic sheets and then with drop cloths, to protect them from spatters. Next, strip the room of all light fixtures, switch and outlet plates, heat registers—anything that can get in the way of a brush or roller head. As you remove small items, put them into plastic bags and label the bags by location. For large items with small parts, such as drapery rods, put the components into plastic bags and tape them to the host item. Drop ceiling lights and chandeliers away from the ceiling and cover them with plastic lawn bags.

When the room is cleared, thoroughly vacuum the floor if it is carpeted; damp-mop if it has a hard surface. Vacuum or wipe down the baseboards. Then stick strips of 1½-inch-wide blue masking tape, sometimes called painter's tape, around the perimeter of the floor, butting the strips tightly to the baseboards. Cut strips of 2-mil plastic sheeting to cover the floor, fitting them against each wall, and seal these strips to the blue masking tape with standard masking tape. Make the strips snug but not taut. Then cover the plastic with drop cloths anchored to the sheeting with double-backed tape. The cloths will absorb paint and provide a nonskid surface on which to walk—the plastic would be too slippery otherwise.

To make cleanup easier, professional painters line a bucket with a number of 13-gallon plastic bags. They toss scraps of loose paint or wallpaper into it as they work, removing each bag as it gets full. When the job is done, they remove the drop cloths, then toss the filled debris bags, disposable brushes, steel wool, and all other debris onto the plastic sheeting on the floor and roll it into a ball for easy disposal. *Note:* Chemicals such as paint stripper are not harmful to the environment once they are dry.

Tool Checklist

As you read through this chapter, check this list for items that you will need to clean, repair, and smooth surfaces. Many of the larger items are available from tool rental agencies.

- Broad knives, 6- and 10-inch
- Broom or dust mop
- Can opener, punch type
- Brushes, disposable
- Brushes, soft (3-inch or available paintbrushes)
- Clamps (for scaffolding)
- Drop cloths
- Eye protection
- Garden sprayer
- Gloves, latex and surgical
- Heat gun, electric
- Ladders and plank
- Nail set
- Nylon pot scrubber
- Pails or buckets: 1-quart, 1-gallon, 5-gallon
- Paint scrapers, hooked and straightedged
- Perforation tool
- Plaster washers
- Plastic bags: 30-gallon lawn bags with pull handles, 13- or 15-gallon kitchen bags, 1-quart self-sealing food storage bags
- Plastic sheeting, 2-mil
- Pole sander, extendible
- Power drill with propeller
- Power sander, palm finish sander, or half-sheet orbital sander
- Power screwdriver
- Putty knife, 2-inch
- Respirator
- Roller covers, disposable
- Sandpaper, various grits
- Sponge mop, household
- Sponges, preferably those made for tile work
- Steel wool: various grades, including #0 and #0000
- Tack cloth
- Tape: 2-inch standard masking tape, 1½-inch blue (painter's) masking tape, and 2- or 3-inch double-backed tape
- Tape, wallboard (fiberglass or paper)
- Vacuum cleaner, with attachments
- Wallboard sanding screen
- Wallboard saw
- Wallboard screws, various sizes
- Wire brushes: coarse with 2-mil bristles, and fine with brass bristles

Materials for Prepping

These materials fall into three broad categories: removal agents, preparation and patching products, and sealers.

The removal agents include chemical paint removers to strip paint, enzyme-based wallpaper removers to strip wallcoverings, denatured alcohol to neutralize chemically stripped areas, and mineral spirits and wood cleaners to clean varnished and waxed wood surfaces. This category also includes these household products: liquid fabric softener, white vinegar, baking soda, dish-washing detergent, and petroleum jelly (to create a buffer between surgical gloves and latex gloves).

The preparation and patching products include wallboard compounds to patch and seal wallboard surfaces, self-adhesive fiberglass mesh tapes and patches, paper joint tapes to repair wallboard, patching plasters to repair large defects in plaster surfaces, lightweight interior vinyl spackling pastes to repair small defects in wallboard and plaster, latex wood putties to repair varnished wood surfaces, caulks to seal seams between woodwork and walls, liquid paint deglossers to dull glossy surfaces, and

Tools of preparation: At top left are a 6-foot step ladder, a 2 by 12 plank, folded drop cloths, trash bags (13- and 30-gallon), and a step stool. In front of the stool are a sponge mop, 5-gallon and 2-gallon buckets, latex gloves, a tile sponge, and a stirring stick. In front of the ladder are tools for removing wallpaper: a pump sprayer, scouring sponge, and two perforators. In front of the vacuum cleaner are sanding tools: a pole sander, palm-held power sander, orbital power sander, sanding block, dust mask, goggles, sanding sponges, cheesecloth, sanding screens, and sandpaper.

At bottom right *are a heat gun, coarse wire brush, paint scraper, fine wire brush, and nylon brush.* At bottom left *are disposable foam brushes, bristle brushes, and rollers for applying primer.* At left center *are wallboard screws, a can opener, two nail sets, a 1½-inch putty knife, 5-inch taping knife, 8-inch taping knife, and mud tray.* In the center *are tools for stripping woodwork: a bucket, chemical stripper, surgical gloves, steel wool, and scouring sponges. Below the stripping tools are ¾- and 1½-inch blue tape, 3-inch masking tape, and masking film.*

latex bonding agents to make plaster repairs secure.

Sealers are essentially base-coat products that close the surface pores in repaired spots so the primer can bond firmly. These products include white-pigmented shellacs, oil-based undercoats, and sanding sealers.

Ladders

For most homeowners, two sturdy 6-foot stepladders and a 12-foot-long 2 by 10 plank work quite well. If you have only one stepladder, borrow another one. To reach ceilings, turn the ladders so the steps face one another and run the plank between them so it extends 1 foot beyond each ladder's back legs. For stairwells, run the plank through one stepladder to a step. The plank should be level, reach to the back of the stair tread, and extend 1 foot beyond the ladder's back legs. Keep the plank close to the wall, and secure it with clamps.

If stepladders make you nervous, use platform ladders and an 8-foot-long plank in the same way. A platform ladder is a sturdy tool that gives you an 18-inch-square surface on which to set your bucket or tray. Its broad steps make it comfortable to stand on.

Professional painters use a 5-foot platform ladder, a four-segment multifunction ladder, and a 10-foot extension ladder to do their work. Combined with an 8-foot-long 2 by 10 plank, these ladders give them all the height they need to paint stairwells, vaulted ceilings, and other high places.

SMOOTHING SURFACES

A truly smooth surface is a must for firm adhesion, a long-lasting finish, and a flawless professional appearance. Two things produce a smooth base: removing any old finish that could interfere with the new one, and repairing all damage and defects. This section presents several techniques for both operations; follow those that pertain to your situation.

Two Professional Techniques

Almost all repairs include patching and sanding. Rather than repeat information on them continually throughout this book, they are presented here so you can learn them before you start.

How to Apply Patching Compounds

Except for tiny repairs, patching should always be done in a crossing pattern. First, fill the void with horizontal strokes, working from the bottom up and from left to right if you are right-handed, the opposite if you are left-handed. When the void has been filled, immediately pull your broad knife down vertically across the damp compound, to skim off any excess. The compound should fill the void flush with the wall surface and should be feathered (tapered to nothing) onto the surrounding wall. You can use a 2-inch putty knife, a 6-inch broad knife, or a 10-inch broad knife to apply these compounds, depending on the size of the repair. Ideally, the knife is wide enough to bridge the damaged area and

smooth it with one pass. If you can't do this, however, don't worry. Use as many strokes as you need to fill and smooth it, aiming to hold down the amount of sanding needed.

If you are filling deep holes, it is better to apply the compound in 2 or more layers, to avoid shrinking or slumping. Apply a thick coat first, to within ⅛ inch of the finished surface. Don't smooth it; leave it rough and let it dry overnight. Then apply the second, final, coat as described.

How to Sand Correctly

Sanding is important to producing a flawless finish. It should be done after each step in a repair. In most situations, sand lightly, rubbing just enough to remove peaks of patching material and lightly polish the surface. You can use a wallboard sanding screen, a handheld sanding block, or a pole sander to do most jobs. Use a power sander for large areas—a palm sander or a half-sheet orbital sander work best. Do not use a power belt sander; it will abrade the surface too much. Be careful not to dig into the surface as you sand. Sand wallboard and plaster along the longest

Top: For large cracks and small holes, apply patching compound over a fiberglass backing. Follow up with two or three more layers, each feathered beyond the previous layer and sanded smooth.
Bottom: Finish by priming and painting.

Floating a Wall

Scraping loose paint

Sanding

Pole sander

Applying shellac

Applying compound

10" knife

direction; sand wood with the grain. Always wear a respirator, and seal the room off from other rooms.

Prepping Painted Surfaces

All chipped, peeling, or flaking paint should be completely removed. If it isn't, it will create unsightly spots under your new finish and keep the finish from bonding firmly with the underlying surface. Particularly in older homes, surfaces coated with many layers of paint may peel, or the house may have textured walls and ceilings you don't want. In these situations, especially with peeling paint that may contain lead (see page 26) give the walls a new surface. You want to seal any lead-based paint behind an impregnable cover.

How to Smooth Painted Walls and Ceilings

There are four ways to smooth walls and ceilings. One is to tear out the existing surface and hang new wallboard—a messy, expensive, time-consuming process.

Another is to glue and screw ¼-inch-thick sheets of new wallboard to the old walls and ceiling. If you have plaster walls and ceilings, this method lets you install a much-needed plastic vapor barrier before you install the new wallboard. However, this form of encapsulation has a major disadvantage: You have to remove all the woodwork before you hang the wallboard and then reinstall it when you are done.

A third solution is to float defective walls and ceilings. Floating, or mudding, is covering surfaces with a thin, smooth coating of plaster, joint compound, or similar material.

A fourth way to smooth walls, if they have been roughened by textured paint, is to strip off the textured paint.

Floating Peeling Walls and Ceilings

This is a quick, reliable, inexpensive, and fairly easy way to stabilize and seal off a peeling or rough surface. It takes part of three days. Be sure to wear a respirator for all scraping and sanding operations.

1. Scrape away the peeling paint with a 6-inch broad knife or wire brush. Be careful not to mar the surface. Do not scrape textured surfaces; see the following section for information on how to deal with them.

2. Sand the entire surface with a pole sander and 40-grit sandpaper. Dust down the area with a clean broom or dust mop. Damp-mop to pick up all the paint dust.

3. Apply one coat of white-pigmented shellac to the wall, using a disposable brush or a roller with a disposable cover. Let it dry, which will take 45

minutes to 1 hour. Sand lightly with 100-grit sandpaper. Clean up the sanding dust. Apply a second coat of shellac and let it dry. Sand with 120-grit sandpaper.

4. Thin premixed joint compound with water until it is the consistency of frosting. A drill with a propeller is the best tool for this job.

5. Before applying compound, visually divide each surface into 4-foot-square sections.

6. Apply the compound to the 4 by 4 sections in a pattern of large sweeping strokes.

To float walls, start in a corner at the bottom of the lower half of a wall and, using a 10-inch broad knife, apply the joint compound to the first 4 by 4 section of wall. Repeat this process on each adjoining 4 by 4 section until the lower half of the wall is covered. Return to the starting corner and float the top half of the wall in the same way (see photograph, page 28). Let the compound dry overnight.

To float a ceiling, use the same technique, starting in the corner at one end of the room. Cover the first row of 4 by 4 sections across the narrow width of the room; then work the next row of 4 by 4 sections, and so on until the ceiling is covered. Again, let the compound dry overnight.

7. Sand the surface with 120-grit sandpaper. Vacuum and damp-mop to remove all sanding dust.

8. Apply a second coat of joint compound in the same way, smoothing as much as possible with the vertical strokes to minimize sanding. Let dry overnight.

9. Sand with 120-grit sandpaper. Vacuum and damp-mop to remove all sanding dust.

10. Seal with a coat of oil-based undercoat.

Stripping Textured Paints

There are four ways to smooth walls covered with textured paint. If you are going to use a wallcovering, you can cover the surface with liner paper (see page 75), but this works only marginally well, and only if the texture isn't too coarse. You can cover the old walls with new ¼-inch wallboard. Or you can float them as described on page 25. The fourth, and easiest, solution is to strip off the textured paint. This is a messy but simple five-step process that uses an effective homemade remover. To make the remover, mix 1 gallon water, 2 cups liquid fabric softener (any brand), 1 cup white vinegar, and 1 bottle wallpaper remover with reactive enzymes (the label should state that the remover is enzyme-based). Apply this solution to the textured paint with a garden sprayer, as follows.

1. Start in one corner and work your way around the room in orderly sections. Spray a fine mist of the remover on the wall in each section, working from the baseboard to the ceiling. Let stand 5 minutes. Spray again in the same direction. Let stand 5 minutes more and spray a third time. Let stand another 5 minutes.

2. With a 6-inch broad knife, strip off the textured paint, working from the bottom up. Scrape gently so you don't mar the surface.

3. With a clean sponge or sponge mop, wipe down the

What to Do About Lead Paint and Asbestos

When you remove paint in an older home, you risk releasing two hazardous substances into the air: lead and asbestos.

Lead

Lead is poisonous to everyone, but it is especially harmful to children—even minute amounts can damage their brains. Most paint manufactured before 1950 contained large amounts of lead. With the development of latex paints in 1950, the amount of lead-based paints used in American homes steadily dropped. However, it took a good fifteen years for latex to become the standard interior paint. The federal government set lead limits for other paints in 1978. This means that if your home contains paint manufactured before 1978, it may have lead; if it contains paint manufactured before 1965, it probably does; if it

contains paint manufactured before 1950, it definitely does.

The problem arises when lead-based paints begin to chip off or peel away. Children may pick up and chew these pieces. Also, as the paint disintegrates, it creates a lead dust that can contaminate your house. This is why the U.S. Department of Health has called for the removal of all loose or degraded lead-based paint from America's homes. Be careful to remove this paint in a way that does not produce lead debris, dust, and fumes that can be swallowed or inhaled. Authorities recommend four ways to do this job.
•Dry scraping (see opposite page): As you scrape away the paint, mist the surface lightly to hold down dust. Wear a respirator, and thoroughly wet-mop the area to remove all lead dust when done. Don't vacuum—that just spreads the lead dust.

•Sealing, or encapsulation: Cover the peeling walls with wallboard or paneling, or float them with wallboard compound (see page 25).
•Replacement: Remove all surfaces coated with lead-based paint and install new surfaces in their place. This includes walls, woodwork, and window and door frames.
•Chemical paint removers (see opposite page): If used correctly, chemical strippers don't produce lead dust.

Sanding and sandblasting are not recommended because they produce dust. Heat guns are not recommended because they can produce toxic lead fumes.

Asbestos
Asbestos fibers can cause a number of serious lung diseases. Any home built before 1970 probably contains building materials made with asbestos—anything from sheet

flooring to textured ceiling sprays—but this is not an automatic cause for alarm. Authorities say such materials don't pose a hazard to human health if they are in good condition; the fibers are solidly encased and cannot be released into the air. Their advice? Leave such materials alone. Disturbing them is far more hazardous than living with them.

A problem can occur, however, if asbestos fibers break loose when you sand or scrape surfaces such as spray-textured ceilings. If you must change such surfaces, cover them with wallboard (usually ¼-inch), float them with joint compound, or hire an asbestos abatement contractor to remove and replace them.

Contact your state or county health department for more specific information about how to handle lead and asbestos in your home.

stripped walls with the remover to dislodge remaining bits of paint.

4. To rinse, combine 1 gallon water with ¼ cup white vinegar; use a sponge or sponge mop to apply. Let dry.

5. Seal the walls with a coat of white-pigmented shellac, using a disposable brush or roller cover.

About Textured Ceilings

A textured ceiling, especially one that was sprayed before 1970, could contain asbestos. For that reason alone, you should not attempt to remove the texture in the same way you can remove textured paint from walls. The binder used with sprayed ceiling materials is not nearly so stable as that in textured paint. Scraping the texture off a ceiling may release asbestos fibers into your home environment.

If you are determined to have a smooth ceiling, you have three choices: (1) Cover the ceiling with wallboard. (2) Float, or mud, the ceiling as described on the opposite page, without scraping off the texture. (3) Hire an asbestos abatement contractor to remove and replace the ceiling material.

How to Strip Wood

You can strip paint or varnish from woodwork and paneling by dry scraping, or by using a chemical paint remover or an electric heat gun to soften the finish and then scraping. The method you use depends on the size and number of chipped spots and the type of finish you will be applying.

Dry Scraping

Scraping, followed by a light sanding, is the best way to strip woodwork with few or small damaged areas, especially if you are going to apply the same type of finish. Your goal is to remove all the loose paint down to a smooth surface.

1. With a hooked paint scraper or wire brush, scrape away all the visibly loose paint. Work from the bottom up. Scrape well back into the sound paint because paint around the edges of a damaged area can be loose even if it isn't visibly pulling away.

2. Use the scraper, followed by 100-grit sandpaper, to feather the edges of the spot into the existing paint. The surface should be smooth to the touch, and flush.

3. Seal with one coat of shellac: white-pigmented shellac if the woodwork is to be painted, clear shellac if it is to be varnished. Let dry.

Chemical Stripping

If the existing paint is layered thickly, or if large sections are damaged, or if you are going to change the finish (from paint to varnish, for example), you need to remove the finish down to the bare wood. Use a chemical paint remover to do a job of this size. *Caution:*

Paint-stripping chemicals are highly caustic. This can't be emphasized strongly enough. Wear protective gear, including safety goggles, a respirator, plastic apron, knee covers, and latex gloves. Professional painters put on a pair of surgical gloves, wet their gloved hands with water or rub on a coat of petroleum jelly, then slip them into a pair of latex gloves. This creates a strong barrier to the caustic chemical. Follow the remover manufacturer's directions for safe and effective use, and always work in a well-ventilated area.

There are three steps to chemical stripping.

1. Work in 1-foot-square sections. Use a disposable brush. Brush a thick coat of the stripper in one direction over the painted surface. Do not brush back and forth—this will reduce the chemical's effectiveness. Let the stripper stand for the recommended time, plus 10 minutes, during which time the softened paint will form an easily removed layer. Apply another coat if it dries out.

2. Scrape away as much of the softened paint as possible with #0 steel wool, a putty knife, or a nylon pot scrubber. Change to a new steel wool when one becomes clogged; rinse the pot scrubber in a bucket containing 2 gallons water and 2 cups white vinegar.

3. Rub the cleaned surface with #0000 steel wool and denatured alcohol to remove the last bits of paint and neu-tralize the surface. Rub with the grain of the wood. Let dry for at least 24 hours.

Heat-Gun Stripping

Softening paint with an electric heat gun is not generally recommended because it is tedious, dangerous, and less effective than chemical paint removers. In addition, it leaves paint embedded in the wood grain, which you have to remove with a chemical stripper. However, if you insist on using a heat gun, wear heavy leather work gloves, a respirator, and goggles, and follow the manufacturer's directions for how long and how close to hold the gun to the surface. You don't want to scorch the wood or set the paint on fire. *Caution:* Never use a heat gun on wood that has been treated with a chemical stripper or on a surface covered with lead paint.

The final 4-by-4-foot section of this wall, also shown on the front cover, is being floated with a thin layer of joint compound. The wall was sealed with white shellac first. See Floating Peeling Walls and Ceilings, page 25.

Stripping Cabinets

Most kitchen cabinets are coated with factory-applied, heat-cured epoxy finishes that cannot be stripped with ordinary chemical paint removers. Try to do this and you'll have a mess on your hands. If you must refinish your cabinets, sand them just enough to break the surface glaze, and then paint them the desired color, applying the paint in two light coats (see page 51).

Removing Old Wallcoverings

There are several reasons why you shouldn't paint or paper over an old wallcovering. The covering may not be adhering well to the wall; when the new paint or adhesive wets it, it can pull away; dyes in the wallpaper may bleed through the new finish; and paint and paper cannot adhere to many wallcovering surfaces, including flocks and foils. If at all possible, remove old wallcoverings before you refinish the walls.

How to Remove Wallcoverings

If the wallcovering is a strip-pable paper and it was applied correctly, it should simply pull away from the wall. If necessary, soften paste residue with a sponge and hot water. Use a 6-inch broad knife to remove the residue. For other coverings, manufactured wallpaper removers or a wallpaper steamer can help soften the paper's adhesive so the paper can be scraped from the wall, but these methods are cumbersome at best. If the wallpaper wasn't applied correctly, they may not work at all. The best method for removing any wallcovering, no matter how it was applied or how many layers there are, even if they are covered with layers of paint, is the following technique.

1. Make a remover by combining 3 gallons very hot water (as hot as possible), 1 bottle wallpaper remover with reactive enzymes (the label should state it is enzyme-based), ¼ cup liquid fabric softener (any brand), and 2 tablespoons baking soda.

2. If the wallcovering has a water-resistant or nonporous vinyl surface, use a perforation tool, wire brush, or 60-grit sandpaper to break the surface so the remover can get to the adhesive. If you sand, work the block or palm sander in a circular motion, applying just enough pressure to score the surface.

3. Pour 1 gallon of the remover into a clean (not used for garden chemicals) garden sprayer. Spray a fine mist of the remover on the walls, working from the bottom to the ceiling, one section at a time. When you've sprayed all the walls, immediately spray them again in the same manner and order, and then immediately spray a third time. Take a 15-minute break to let the solution work.

4. Using a 6-inch broad knife, scrape each strip of wallcovering off the wall, working from the bottom up. They'll slip off easily. Work around the room in the same order you applied the remover.

5. Spray the stripped walls with the remaining remover; wipe them down with a sponge or sponge mop to remove all adhesive residue.

6. Rinse the walls with a neutralizing solution of 1 cup white vinegar in 1 gallon water.

Removing Wallcoverings

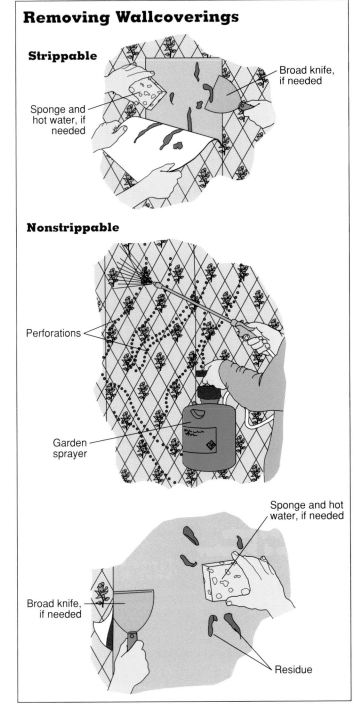

Strippable

Broad knife, if needed

Sponge and hot water, if needed

Nonstrippable

Perforations

Garden sprayer

Sponge and hot water, if needed

Broad knife, if needed

Residue

Repairing Walls, Ceilings, and Woodwork

After removing old finishes, repair all imperfections, no matter how minor.

How to Repair Wallboard

Wallboard can develop cracks, especially at stress points, but the big problems are popped nails, holes, and open joints.

Fixing Popped Nails

The normal expansion and contraction of a house cause some wallboard nails to pop out over time. Fix them with this five-step method.

1. Drive a 1¼-inch wallboard screw into the stud or joist, about 2 inches from the popped nail and 1/32 inch below the wallboard surface. The screw should pull the wallboard tight against the framing.

2. Remove the popped nail and scrape away any loose material.

3. With a 6-inch broad knife, cover the nail hole and screw head with premixed joint compound. Let dry overnight; then apply a thin second coat. Let it dry overnight. Then apply a thin third, or finish, coat. Let dry overnight.

4. Sand the patches with 120-grit sandpaper.

5. Seal each patch with white-pigmented shellac.

Filling Small Spots

If the paper around the edges of the blemished area is not broken, fill the spot with a general-purpose interior spackling paste applied with a 2-inch putty knife. Let dry,

which will take 10 to 40 minutes. Sand with 120-grit sandpaper. If the paper is broken or the edges cracked, cover the area with self-adhesive fiberglass mesh tape or moistened paper joint tape and apply patching compound (see page 24).

Patching Medium and Large Holes

You will have to make a backing or use a patch large enough to span two or more studs; then you can patch the hole.

1. Measure the hole.

2. *For a medium hole,* out of scrap wallboard cut a patch that is double the size of the hole. Center the patch over the hole and, with a pencil, trace around the patch. With a wallboard saw cut out the marked area, making the incision just outside the pencil line. *For a large hole,* cut out enough wallboard to span at least 2 studs.

3. *For a medium hole,* cut 1 or more backer strips out of plywood, 1-by boards, or wallboard scraps. They should be 3 to 4 inches wider than the hole. Slip them behind the opening and secure them to the wall with 1¼-inch wallboard screws.

4. *For a medium hole,* lightly coat the edges of the hole and the patch with joint compound. Push the patch into the opening and use 1¼-inch wallboard screws to fasten it to the backer strips. *For a large hole,* nail or screw the patch to the studs.

5. Apply strips of self-adhesive fiberglass mesh tape or moistened paper joint tape to the seams of the patch, overlapping the tape at the ends.

6. Work a coat of joint compound into and over the tape,

Patching Small Holes

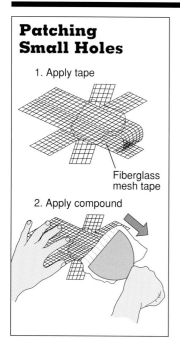

1. Apply tape

Fiberglass mesh tape

2. Apply compound

Patching Larger Holes

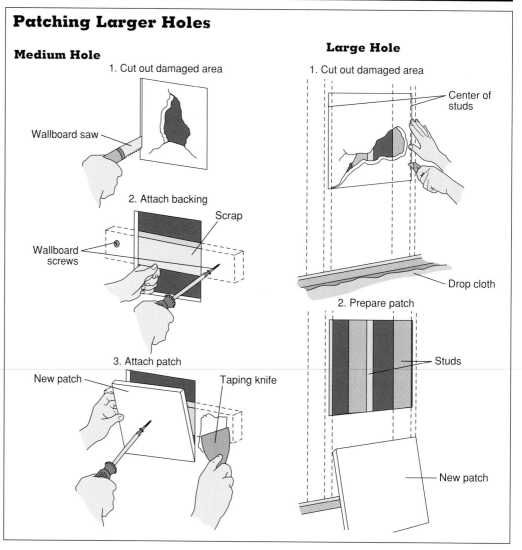

Medium Hole

1. Cut out damaged area

Wallboard saw

2. Attach backing

Wallboard screws

Scrap

3. Attach patch

New patch

Taping knife

Large Hole

1. Cut out damaged area

Center of studs

Drop cloth

2. Prepare patch

Studs

New patch

---

using the crisscrossing technique (see page 24). Let dry overnight.

7. Skim a second coat of compound over the entire patch. Let dry completely.

8. Sand with 120-grit sandpaper.

9. Seal with white-pigmented shellac.

Filling Open Joints

Stress-point cracks are hard to repair because they can reappear when the house shifts again. The secret to filling such cracks is to use an interior vinyl spackling paste, which remains flexible and will expand and contract with the house.

1. If the crack is more than a hairline fissure but narrower than ¼ inch, widen it slightly and undercut its sides with a punch-type can opener. If the crack is wider than ¼ inch, leave it alone. Whatever the size, vacuum, sponge, or brush out the crack to remove all loose debris.

2. With a 6-inch broad knife, apply interior vinyl spackling paste, using the crisscrossing technique (see page 24). Let dry overnight.

3. Sand with 120-grit sandpaper.

4. Reinforce the patched joint along its entire length with self-adhesive fiberglass mesh or moistened paper joint tape. Using a 6-inch broad knife, apply more of the spackling paste over the tape, using the crisscrossing technique. Let dry 10 to 40 minutes. If necessary, sand again

and apply a third coat with a wider knife.

5. Smooth the patch with a damp sponge.

6. Seal the repair with white-pigmented shellac.

How to Repair Damaged Plaster

Extensive damage, or areas larger than 12 inches square, should be repaired by a professional plasterer, or the wall or ceiling should be covered with wallboard. With smaller cracks and holes, the lath provides a backing for the patch-

ing material. However, many plastered surfaces have a texture that must be matched after the repair is made. If you are repairing such a surface, scrape away the texture before you begin. You can match it when you paint (see page 53).

Fixing Cracks and Small Holes

Repair cracks, and holes less than 3 inches square, by filling them with interior vinyl spackling paste. First, test the plaster around the defect for soundness. If it is sound, proceed with the repair outlined here. If it isn't, use a scraper to remove the weakened spots, working outward until only a sound surface remains. Now proceed with the repair as follows.

1. Clean out any loose material with a putty knife or linoleum knife. Dust with a clean paintbrush.

2. Dampen the surface around the defect with a latex bonding agent, following the manufacturer's directions, or with water to which you have added a drop of dish-washing detergent.

3. If the repair is a tiny nail hole or hairline crack, use a 2-inch putty knife to fill it with interior vinyl spackling paste. One coat should be sufficient. *For larger defects,* up to 3 inches square, apply and smooth the interior vinyl spackling paste with a 6-inch broad knife. One coat should be enough unless the crack is quite deep. *For deep cracks,* apply 3 layers of interior vinyl spackling paste. The first layer should be ¼ inch deep, and each additional layer ⅛ inch deep. Allow each coat to dry thoroughly, 10 to 40 minutes, before applying the next.

4. When the last coat is dry, sand with 120-grit sandpaper. Dust clean.

5. Seal the patch with white-pigmented shellac.

Repairing Defects Up to 12 Inches Square

Use patching plaster (not spackling paste or wallboard joint compound) to repair large holes and cracks. Start by testing the surrounding plaster for soundness. If it is sound, proceed with the repair outlined here. If it isn't, scrape or chisel away the damaged plaster until only a sound surface remains, then proceed. If necessary, secure the sound plaster around damaged areas with wallboard screws and plaster washers before removing damaged plaster.

1. Remove loose material, using a putty knife or chisel. Dust the entire area with a clean paintbrush. Dampen the edges with water to which a drop of dish-washing detergent has been added, or apply a latex bonding agent according to the manufacturer's directions.

2. Mix the patching plaster until it is smooth and thick like heavy oatmeal.

3. For shallow holes (less than ¼ inch deep), use a 10-inch broad knife to apply the plaster. One layer should be sufficient. *For deeper holes,* apply a heavy base layer to within ¼ inch of the surface, holding the broad knife at a 45-degree angle as you press the plaster against the lath. Let the plaster set for 15 minutes, then with a nail or knife blade score it at ½-inch intervals in a crosshatch pattern. Let set overnight.

4. Apply a second layer of patching plaster over the first, almost to the final surface. Let set for 1 hour.

5. Mix some patching plaster with water until it is creamy. Apply this finish coat over the base coats, making it as smooth as possible. Let set for 30 minutes to 1 hour.

6. Smooth the patch with a damp sponge to eliminate sanding, then let harden completely.

7. Seal the patch with white-pigmented shellac.

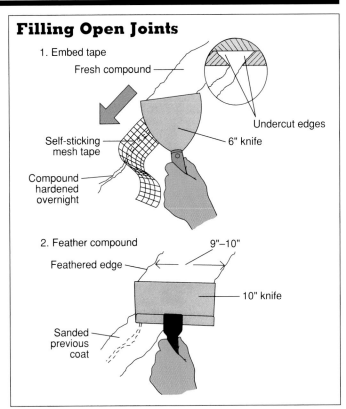

Filling Open Joints

1. Embed tape

Fresh compound

Self-sticking mesh tape

Compound hardened overnight

Undercut edges

6" knife

2. Feather compound

Feathered edge

9"–10"

10" knife

Sanded previous coat

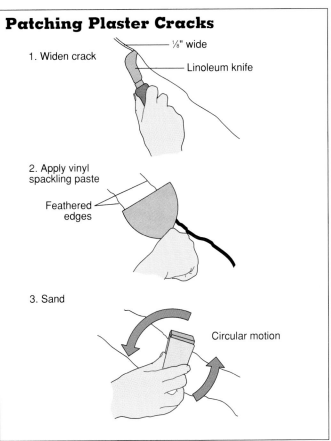

Patching Plaster Cracks

1. Widen crack

⅛" wide

Linoleum knife

2. Apply vinyl spackling paste

Feathered edges

3. Sand

Circular motion

Repairing Sagging Plaster

Gently probe the loose area of plaster. If it is firm and doesn't break with your probing, you can secure it to the lath with 1½-inch wallboard screws and special plaster washers.

1. Thread the washers onto the screws. With a power screwdriver, drive the screws into the lath behind the weakened area until the washers are slightly embedded in the plaster. Space the screws 4 inches apart, and screw into a stud or joist as often as possible.

2. With a 2-inch putty knife, cover the exposed washers with interior vinyl spackling paste. Let dry for about 40 minutes.

3. Sand with 120-grit sandpaper.

4. Seal the repair with white-pigmented shellac.

Patching Plaster Holes

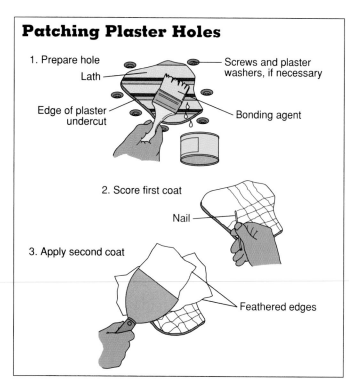

1. Prepare hole
Lath
Edge of plaster undercut
Screws and plaster washers, if necessary
Bonding agent

2. Score first coat
Nail

3. Apply second coat
Feathered edges

Securing Loose Plaster

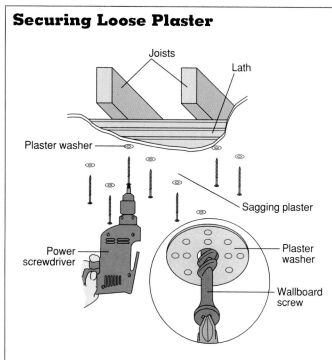

Joists
Lath
Plaster washer
Power screwdriver
Sagging plaster
Plaster washer
Wallboard screw

How to Repair Damaged or Bare Woodwork

Clean, repair, and sand all woodwork before applying any finish. If you have scraped and smoothed the damaged spots or stripped off the old finish, you have already completed the first step of this process. Preparation for painting or sealing bare woodwork, including window and door frames, is the same.

Preparing Woodwork to Be Painted

If the existing finish is sound or its rough areas have been scraped and sanded until smooth, proceed with step 1. If all the finish has been stripped off or if the trim is new bare wood, start with step 3.

1. Wash the woodwork with water and a low-phosphate multipurpose household cleaner. Rinse with clean water. Buff dry with a soft, clean towel.

2. If the trim is painted with a glossy enamel, wipe it down with a liquid deglosser, following the manufacturer's instructions, or sand it with 150-grit sandpaper to dull the shiny surface.

3. Apply latex wood putty to damaged spots. Caulk all seams between the trim and the wall; reset glazing putty if necessary. Let dry 24 hours.

4. Sand patched areas with 150-grit sandpaper.

5. Seal patches with white-pigmented shellac. It will dry in about 1 hour.

6. Sand entire surface with 150-grit sandpaper. Vacuum and then lightly wipe the surface with a tack cloth to pick up all dust.

7. Seal entire surface with white-pigmented shellac.

Preparing Woodwork to Be Clear-Sealed

If the existing finish is sound or its rough areas have been scraped and sanded until smooth, proceed with step 1. If the finish has been completely stripped off or the woodwork is new bare wood, start with step 2.

1. Clean the woodwork with a soft cloth and odorless mineral spirits, wood cleaner, or furniture refinisher. Let dry.

2. With a 2-inch putty knife, apply stainable latex wood putty to all holes and other defects. Let dry 30 minutes. Caulk the seams between the trim and the wall and restore the glazing compound around the window panes if needed.

3. Sand patched areas with 150-grit sandpaper. Then lightly sand the entire surface. Vacuum, then wipe with a tack cloth to pick up dust.

4. Stain patched areas, or the entire surface if it is new bare wood, as desired.

5. When stain has set, apply one coat of sanding sealer.

CLEANING SURFACES

A clean surface is just as crucial to adhesion and proper coverage as a smooth surface. Clean means the surface is free of stains, dirt, grease, and dust. Scrubbing walls and woodwork may be dreary tasks, but they are necessary for a successful job of either painting or wallcovering.

Scrubbing Walls and Ceilings

Walls and ceilings are coated with more than dust. They have a greasy film that must be removed before you paint or wallpaper. This film does not mean you are a bad housekeeper. It is a normal by-product of people living in an enclosed environment, although such things as frying foods and cigarette smoke will make it worse. You must remove this film from your walls and ceilings (you've already taken it off your woodwork; see opposite page) if you want your paint or wallcovering to bond well to these surfaces.

First, dust all surfaces by using a vacuum cleaner and its soft-brush attachment or by sweeping them with a clean broom or dust mop. Use the crevice attachment or a small, soft brush to vacuum dust from corners and crevices. Then, wash the walls with a low-phosphate multipurpose household cleaner, mixed according to the manufacturer's directions, or with this homemade cleaning solution: 1 gallon water, ½ cup low-phosphate trisodium phosphate (TSP) substitute, and 2 tablespoons liquid fabric softener (any brand).

Wear latex gloves. Pour the cleaning solution into a garden sprayer. Spray one wall at a time with a fine mist of the cleaner. Let stand for 5 minutes. Then, using a clean sponge or a sponge mop, scrub the wall from the bottom up. Use the rough edge of the mop head for stubborn spots. Wash a smooth ceiling the same way. Do not attempt to scrub a ceiling covered with textured acoustical spray (see page 27).

Rinse the walls and ceiling in the same order you sprayed them, using a solution of ¼ cup white vinegar in 1 gallon water. Use a fresh gallon for each wall. Use a clean sponge mop to brush on and pick up the rinse water. *Note:* If you use a multipurpose household cleaner that says it doesn't have to be rinsed, rinse anyway.

While scrubbing these surfaces, you may encounter stains and other problems that require a special removal technique.

Mildew

Mildew and mold look like splotches of dirt. They are caused by fungi that thrive in warm, damp rooms with poor ventilation. Wet a rag with a small amount of chlorine

bleach and dab it on the spot. If the splotch comes off, it's mold or mildew. You must get rid of it; it will come through paint and other finishes. Prepare a solution of 2 teaspoons dishwashing detergent, ⅔ cup baking soda, 1 cup chlorine bleach, and 1 gallon water. This will kill the spores. Effective commercial mildew-removing cleaners also are available. Wear latex gloves and goggles. Apply the solution with a damp mop and let set for several minutes. Then rinse the area thoroughly with a solution of ¼ cup white vinegar in 1 gallon water and allow it to dry. Lightly sand the spot and seal it against reinfection by applying 2 coats of white-pigmented shellac, allowing the first coat to dry completely before applying the second. Sand between coats. For long-range prevention, improve the room's ventilation.

Grease-Based Stains

Some grease stains may not come off when you wash the wall. To remove them, rub them with liquid deglosser to break the oil film. When the spot is dry, lightly sand it with 120-grit paper. Clean up the sanding dust and apply 2 coats of white-pigmented shellac. Allow the first coat to dry completely, about 1 hour, before applying the second coat. Sand between coats.

Water or Rust Stains

These stains indicate water damage. Locate and eliminate the source before you treat the stain. Make sure the stained

surface is completely dry. Dig out and repair any disintegrated areas, using the repair methods described on pages 29 to 32. Add 2 tablespoons baking soda to 1 gallon water and use this solution to scrub the area. Allow to dry for several days, then sand with 120-grit sandpaper and seal with 2 coats of white-pigmented shellac. Allow the first coat to dry completely, about 1 hour, before applying the second coat. Sand between coats.

Sanding Walls and Ceilings

Walls and ceilings coated with a flat paint that has been scrubbed with a low-phosphate cleaner do not need to be sanded. However, surfaces covered with a semigloss or gloss paint should be lightly sanded after they are cleaned and before you apply the new finish. Use a 150-grit sandpaper if the gloss has a low or medium sheen. A liquid deglosser can be used in place of the sandpaper or in areas hard to reach with sandpaper. Apply it according to the manufacturer's directions. Surfaces with a high sheen should be sanded twice: first with 120-grit sandpaper and then with 150-grit sandpaper or liquid deglosser. Wear latex gloves and goggles when using the deglosser. Then rinse the area with 1 gallon water combined with ¼ cup white vinegar. This will remove dust and neutralize the surface.

PAINTING KNOW-HOW

Now the fun begins. Prepping is over. You are about to discover it was time well spent, as your paint spreads on easily and quickly. This is your reward for repairing, smoothing, and scrubbing every surface. You get two other rewards: a flawless finish, and color—color that transforms a dreary room, that makes people feel good, that gives the room personality. Furthermore, thanks to modern chemistry, today's paints do everything you need them to do without special effort on your part. They cover well, protect surfaces from wear, resist discoloration and fading, and apply easily. This chapter presents all you need to know about choosing paint products and mastering a few basic application techniques that will allow you to produce professional-looking results.

This room, decorated by professional designers and artisans and featured in a designer showcase, demonstrates some of the endless effects that paint can produce. From the flawlessly smooth surfaces of the wood trim to the deliberately visible brush strokes on the beams to the subtle depth of the wall color, each surface shows how paint enhances a surface with both color and texture.

BUYING THE RIGHT PAINT AND TOOLS

A successful paint job requires more than a well-prepped surface. It also requires that you use the correct paint and primer for the surface to be coated and that you apply it with the proper tools. Fortunately, meeting these requirements is not complicated, expensive, or difficult. You just need some basic knowledge before you shop.

Which Paint Should You Use?

Area	Best Choice	Acceptable Choice
Ceiling	Flat	Eggshell
Living room	Flat	Eggshell
Hallway	Flat	Eggshell
Bedroom	Flat	Eggshell
Children's room	Eggshell	Semigloss
Bathroom	Semigloss or gloss	Eggshell
Kitchen	Semigloss or gloss	Eggshell
Kitchen cabinets	Semigloss or gloss	Eggshell
Woodwork, windows	Semigloss or gloss	Eggshell

Selecting Interior Paints

Paint is just a mixture of pigments, thinners, and binders. However, these basic ingredients have been put together in an amazing number of combinations. Use the following information, plus advice from your retailer to choose the correct paint for your job.

Latex or Alkyd Paint?

There are two types of interior paint: latex and alkyd. They contain similar pigments but their binders and thinners are different.

Latex paints contain vinyl or acrylic resins, or a combination of the two, as binders. The thinner for a latex paint is water. The type of resin determines paint quality. The best contains 100 percent acrylic resin. A medium-priced latex paint contains a blend of vinyl and acrylic resins. A low-cost latex paint contains 100 percent vinyl resin, which produces the least durable finish.

Alkyd paints contain a number of synthetic resins called "alkyds" and are solvent-thinned. They have replaced the oil-based interior paints. People use the terms *oil-based* and *alkyd* interchangeably, which can be confusing, but just remember that any reference to an oil-based interior paint means an alkyd paint. Some people feel the solvent content of alkyd paints contributes to air pollution (see page 40). If you want to know exactly what a paint contains, ask the paint dealer for the manufacturer's Material Safety Data Sheet.

Both types of paint adhere and cover well and give you a beautiful, durable finish for home interiors. However, latex paints are the more popular choice for interior painting, because they dry quickly and clean up with soap and water. They are also nonflammable and practically odor free. Today there is a latex paint suitable for every type of surface and use. However, gloss latex paints are still not quite as durable as gloss alkyds. Alkyd paints, though, must be cleaned up with a solvent. Also, they tend to sag during application and dry slowly.

The Right Sheen

Whether latex or alkyd, all paints have a sheen. Sheen, the amount of light reflected by the surface of a paint, affects the paint's appearance and performance. Manufacturers use many names to describe the different paint sheens. Whatever the names, most paints fall into four sheen categories.

Flat

Flat paints have a nonreflective, matte finish that helps hide surface imperfections. They are appropriate for walls and ceilings in living rooms, dining rooms, and master bedrooms. However, they absorb grease easily and do not stand up well to frequent scrubbing, so they are a poor choice for high-wear rooms.

Eggshell, or Satin

These paints have a soft luster similar to the sheen on the shell of a fresh egg. They are more durable and stain resistant than flat paints. This makes them suitable for walls in children's rooms, hallways, stairways, family rooms, and bathrooms. They are also suitable for woodwork on which a slight sheen is desired.

Semigloss

With a higher sheen than eggshell paints, semigloss paints are even more stain resistant and easier to clean. They are excellent for walls and woodwork subject to heavy wear and frequent scrubbing: kitchens; bathrooms; hallways; family rooms; children's rooms; and all woodwork, including cabinets.

Gloss Paints

Tougher, more durable, more stain resistant, and easier to clean than all other paints, gloss paints have a hard, shiny surface. This shine highlights surface imperfections. These paints are excellent for kitchen and bathroom walls and all woodwork, including high-wear surfaces like railings, and for cabinets.

What Is Enamel?

A type of paint that can provide a semigloss or gloss sheen, enamel contains more binder, or resin, than other types. Also, its pigments are more finely ground. These two differences give enamels their hard, durable, glossy finish. The stain-resistant and abrasion-resistant finish makes enamels ideal for walls and woodwork in high-traffic areas.

Selecting the Primer or Sealer

Both primers and sealers prepare a surface to receive paint by providing tooth, a slightly coarse surface that holds paint, improving a paint's performance, appearance, and longevity. However, they have slightly different functions. Remember: Sealers seal, primers prepare.

Sealers

Sealers, also called undercoats, form a barrier against moisture and seal highly porous surfaces so they won't suck up paint. Use sealers on the following surfaces.

• Bare open-grained woods such as oak and maple

• Bare woods, such as redwood, that bleed through or stain paint

• Large patches of joint compound or patching plaster

• Masonry surfaces, such as unglazed brick, cinder block, and concrete

• Metal surfaces requiring rust inhibitors to prevent corrosion

Failure to seal these surfaces before painting produces a rough, uneven, dull paint finish, which cannot be improved with additional topcoats. Sealers come in latex and alkyd formulas, but the differences between the two needn't concern you greatly. Today's acrylic latex sealers perform as well as alkyd sealers. You can paint over either type with latex or alkyd paint.

Primers

Primers make a surface more uniform and give it tooth. All unpainted surfaces should be

Top: These paints are of the same color but different sheens: gloss (upper left), eggshell (upper right), semigloss (lower right), and flat (lower left).
Bottom: The flat sheen of the wall paint contributes to the simple, sophisticated serenity of this room.

The Language of Painting

Acrylic   A synthetic resin used as the binder in latex paint. The highest-quality binder available, it makes paint durable and resistant to fading.

Adhesion   The ability of a dried paint to stick to a surface without peeling, flaking, or cracking.

Alkyd   A paint that uses synthetic resins, called alkyds, to bind the pigments and solvents together.

Binder   The liquid that holds a paint's pigments and thinner together to make a spreadable film. The more binder a paint contains, the greater its adhesion and durability. Can be either natural or synthetic. Also called vehicle.

Bite   The ability of a finish to adhere to a surface.

Blue masking tape   A masking tape that can be left in place for up to seven days without leaving a sticky residue. Sometimes called painter's tape. Follow manufacturer's advice about surfaces on which to use the tape. Long Mask™ is a common brand name.

Ceiling paint   A thick, flat paint that is made especially for ceilings. It can be tinted to reduce glare.

Color washing   A decorative paint finish. Made by painting tinted glaze coats over a pale base coat.

Cutting in   Applying a narrow band of paint along the edges and corners of a wall or ceiling, or along the edges of woodwork.

Deglossing   Any means of roughing up a surface before painting. It gives the paint something to bite into, which improves adhesion.

Dragging   A decorative paint finish that creates a striped effect. Made by covering a pale base coat with a tinted glaze and then pulling the glaze off with a tool.

Eggshell   Paint that dries to a soft sheen similar to that found on the shell of a fresh egg. Sometimes called satin.

Enamel   Any paint that has finely ground pigments and a high binder content so it dries to a tough, shiny finish. Enamels can be semigloss or gloss.

Flags   The split ends on paintbrush bristles. They help the bristles hold paint.

Flat   Paint that dries to a matte finish. It doesn't reflect light. Sometimes referred to as matte.

Glaze   A thin mixture of oil, thinner, and alkyd paint that is used to make a transparent coating for decorative finishes. Most are tinted.

Glazing compound   Putty-like material used for sealing the exterior edges of window panes.

Gloss   A paint finish that is hard, durable, and shiny. All paints, including enamel, come in a gloss finish.

Hiding (opacity)   The ability of a paint to cover a surface thoroughly so earlier paint doesn't show through.

Lapmark   A brush mark or roller mark visible after paint dries. A sign of using too much paint or overbrushing.

Latex   A water-based paint containing plasticlike vinyl resin, acrylic resin, or a blend of the two.

Leveling   The ability of a paint to even out on the surface, forming a smooth coat so brush marks or roller marks don't show when it is dry.

Luster   See *Sheen*.

Masking   Protecting an area or surface from paint by covering it with regular masking tape, blue masking tape, or painting tape.

Masking tape   A mildly sticky tape that painters use to mask, or protect, a surface for up to 24 hours. After 24 hours it leaves a sticky residue on surfaces to which it is attached. Cannot be used on wallpaper, bare wallboard, or unpainted ceiling tile.

Matte   See *Flat*.

Mineral spirits   A petroleum-based paint thinner.

Muriatic acid   A diluted form of hydrochloric acid used to clean alkali deposits from masonry.

Painter's tape   See *Blue masking tape*.

Painting tape   A special tape that has a micro-barrier edge so paint can't seep through it or under it. Gives a razor-sharp edge for cut-in work. Easy-Mask™ is a common brand name.

Pigment   The ingredients that give paint its color.

Pouncing   A straight up-and-down movement with a brush, sponge, or other paint applicator. It applies paint without rolling or brushing it over the surface. Used for decorative finishes.

Primer   A coarse base coat designed to help paint adhere to and cover an unpainted surface. There are latex and alkyd primers, as well as specialty primers for metal and other special surfaces.

Rag rolling   A decorative paint finish. Made by using bunched-up or twisted rags to roll a colored glaze over a base coat.

Resin   The substance now used as the binder in most paints. Originally derived from natural sources, resins are now almost always synthetics, such as latex, acrylic latex, and urethanes.

Satin   See *Eggshell*.

Scrubbability   The ability of a paint to stand up to repeated washings without losing its color or thickness. Sometimes called washability.

Sealer   An undercoat used to fill highly porous, unpainted surfaces before they receive a coat of paint. Also called underbody.

Semigloss   A paint finish that has a medium amount of light reflection. All paints, including enamel, come in semigloss finishes.

Sheen   The degree of light reflected by a paint. Also called luster and shine.

Shine   See *Sheen*.

Solvent   A petroleum-based liquid used to thin alkyd paints to the right consistency or to clean alkyd paint from brushes, rollers, and other surfaces.

Spackling paste   An all-purpose patching compound for filling cracks, dents, and holes in plaster, wallboard, and painted woodwork.

Where to Use Primers and Sealers

Surface	Product
New wallboard	Latex primer or polyvinyl acetate (PVA) sealer
New plaster	Latex or alkyd primer
Painted wallboard	Spot-prime stains and repaired patches with white-pigmented shellac; prime old, worn painted surface with latex or alkyd primer
Painted plaster	Same as painted wallboard
Bare wood to be painted	Alkyd enamel sealer or undercoat
Painted wood to be painted	Spot-prime repairs with white-pigmented shellac
Bare wood to be clear-finished	Sanding sealer
Masonry	Alkyd or latex penetrating sealer
Metal	Alkyd enamel sealer or undercoat, with rust inhibitors if needed

Sponging   A decorative paint finish. Made using a sponge to dab colored topcoats on a basecoat.

Stencil   An acetate sheet with cutout patterns used in stenciling.

Stenciling   A decorative paint finish made by dabbing paint through cutouts in a template, or stencil.

Textured paint   Latex paint containing inorganic materials that produce a coarse texture.

Thinner   A liquid used to thin paint to the right consistency for easy spreading. Water is the thinner for latex paint, solvent for alkyd paint.

Tooth   A slightly coarse surface that improves a paint's ability to adhere to it.

Turpentine   A thinner, such as mineral spirits, but derived from pine trees.

Underbody   See *Sealer*.

Uniformity   Even-looking appearance in color and texture.

Vinyl   A class of plastic-like resins used to bind pigments, water, and other ingredients in latex paints, primers, and sealers.

Wash   A thin mixture of latex paint and water. Used to make a transparent coating for decorative finishes.

Washability   The same as scrubbability.

Wet edge   A margin of wet paint or glaze bordering an unpainted section. Leaving a wet edge allows a smooth, seamless blend between sections of work.

primed before they are painted, including old woodwork completely stripped of its former finish. A surface that is already painted should be primed if it has large sections repaired with joint compound or patching plaster, if the existing paint is worn thin and you want to start with a like-new surface, or if the existing surface is painted with a bright or dark color and you want to cover it with a much lighter color. Compared to paint, primer doesn't have to be applied as carefully, it dries faster, and it costs less.

As with sealers, there are latex and alkyd primers. Acrylic latex primers are the easiest, most pleasant, and most convenient to use. They perform as well as alkyd primers, have little odor, and clean up with soap and water. You can paint over both types with either latex or alkyd paint.

Buying Paint

You've decided on the type of paint and the sheen you want. This leaves you with three major decisions: the quality,

the color, and the amount of paint you will buy.

Buy a Premium Paint

Most paint manufacturers make their products in three lines, or grades—a good/ better/best situation. Quality determines the price of each line. Whatever the name, a manufacturer's premium paint contains the most expensive pigments and binders—the solids content of paint—and it contains more of them, up to 45 percent of the contents. Though slightly lower in quality, the midprice line—sometimes called decorator grade—contains a range of pigments and binders like those used in the premium grade. These paints make effective substitutes for premium paint when your budget demands it. The low-priced line—sometimes called professional grade or architectural grade—contains less durable binders and uses clays and other inert ingredients to provide coverage.

Always buy the best paint you can afford. Compared with a low-cost interior paint, a premium finish spreads more easily, spatters less, and levels better (this means brush marks won't show when it is dry). Also, it hides better because it contains more pigment—often, a single coat is sufficient, which saves time and money in the long run. And once dry, the film formed by a premium paint is 50 percent thicker than that of a low-cost paint. The result is a tougher, more durable finish that resists fading, yellowing, staining, and abrasion.

Color Selection

All interior paints come in three color formulations: standard factory finishes, custom-mixed colors, and accent paints.

Standard Factory Finishes

These paints are premixed at the factory. They come only in popular colors, with the selection ranging from limited to generous, depending on the manufacturer. Compared to custom-mixed colors, factory-blended paints are mixed more thoroughly; are more resistant to fading; and are more consistent in color.

Custom-Mixed Colors

These colors are mixed by retail paint dealers, decorating centers, and hardware stores. You choose the color from color chips, and the retailer mixes it by blending together a premixed tinting base and liquid colors. Such custom-mixed colors are usually available only in the premium and decorator paint grades. They offer you the widest possible selection of interior colors—one manufacturer offers 6,134 colors. Today, many paint dealers can custom-mix a color to exactly match a fabric, wallcovering, or other object you plan to use in a room. They use a computerized light beam to analyze the sample material's precise color formula, which can be matched in paint. The sample piece of material must be at least 1 inch square and should not have a nap thicker than that of corduroy fabric.

Accent Colors

These are factory-prepared, pure, solid colors—red, blue, yellow, black, and so on. You mix them with one another to get rich, deep colors. Considered premium coatings, they are very durable and resist fading—useful for a sunny room.

Quantity

Follow these steps to determine how much paint to buy.

1. Measure the length and width of the room and compute its perimeter. If the room is 13 feet wide and 18 feet long, for example, its perimeter is 13 + 13 + 18 + 18 = 62 feet.

2. Multiply the perimeter by the room's height to get square feet of wall space. This sample room is 8 feet high, so its square footage is 62 × 8 = 496 square feet.

3. Subtract 21 square feet for each standard door and 15 square feet for each standard window. This sample room has one door and three windows: 21 + 15 + 15 + 15 = 66 square feet. The final calculation is 496 - 66 = 430 square feet of wall space.

4. Divide the square feet of wall space by 300, the square footage easily covered by a gallon of interior paint, to get the number of gallons needed. In this example, you need 1 gallon plus a little over a quart to paint the walls. Check the paint can label to verify coverage. Although many specify 400 square feet per gallon, you are safer planning on 300

Earth-Friendly Paint

In response to environmental concerns, manufacturers have changed paint formulas in recent years. Modern paints, which apply more easily and last longer than older paints, are more friendly to the environment and user alike. Lead, chromium, and mercury have been removed from almost all consumer paints, and chlorofluorocarbons (CFCs) from aerosol paints. That leaves volatile organic compounds (VOCs) as the remaining environmental problem associated with paint.

VOCs are the petroleum-based solvents used to thin and clean up alkyd paints. They give alkyd paint its spreadable consistency. They also improve its ability to accept color pigments, maintain a durable film, and level well. Latex paints also contain small amounts of solvent. Unfortunately, solvent vapors escape into the atmosphere and become part of a complex chemical reaction that produces ozone, a component of smog. At the time this problem was identified, about 2

percent of the VOCs in the atmosphere came from paint.

Manufacturers have been able to reduce the solvent content in their paints in recent years. Most latex paints now contain no more than 10 percent solvent; many contain only 7 percent, and premium acrylic latex paints contain about 4 percent. The solvent content of alkyd paints has dropped from 50 percent to about 20 percent. More changes are likely in the near future.

Professional Painting Tips

• Paint pipes, wrought-iron balustrades, and other contoured surfaces with a paint glove, or mitt, or an HVLP spray gun.

• Use a beveled paint roller to prevent paint buildup in corners.

• Use a bendable paint pad to paint fixed shutters, radiator fins, and other hard-to-access surfaces.

• Paint heating system registers and grills with aerosol paint.

• Avoid overbrushing enamel paints. Working quickly, apply a generous finish coat, and brush lightly. Do not try to touch up areas you've already painted. If you have problems, let the paint dry, degloss, and repaint.

• Wipe paint off a paint shield after each time you use it.

• Reduce paint odor by stirring a few drops of vanilla

extract into the paint. Commercial paint fragrances can also camouflage normal paint odor.

• Complete a paint job within two weeks. This contributes to adhesion between coats.

• If bristles come off the brush, remove them from the painted surface with eyebrow tweezers or by touching them with the wet brush—they should cling to it. Then wipe the brush with a clean cloth to remove the stray bristles.

• Use painting tape to prevent paint from bleeding under the tape edge. This tape has a unique micro-barrier edge that prevents such seepage, and it won't leave a sticky residue or remove the undersurface when pulled up.

• Use a stenciling brush to work paint into deeply patterned woodwork.

Estimating Surface Area

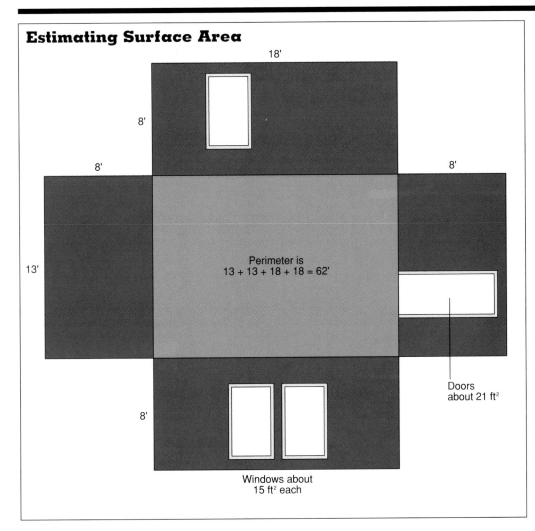

18'

8'

8'   8'

13'

Perimeter is
13 + 13 + 18 + 18 = 62'

Doors
about 21 ft²

8'

Windows about
15 ft² each

square feet so you don't run out in the middle of the job.

Always buy slightly more paint than you need. Since even custom-mixed colors vary slightly from batch to batch, you do not want to be left high and dry with part of the room unpainted. For this sample room you would be wise to buy 1 gallon, 2 quarts rather than 1 gallon, 1 quart. If your computation says you need 3 quarts, round off to a full gallon. This extra allows for spillage, waste, and spots that soak up more paint than expected. Plaster, for example, is more absorbent than wallboard. If the walls are very porous,

divide the square footage by 350 instead of 400. Also, you'll want leftover paint for future touch-ups. Remember to buy extra paint if you plan to paint the interiors of built-in bookshelves or cabinets.

Painting Tools and Equipment

Most interior paint jobs require two or three quality brushes, a paint tray, a roller, and one or two good roller heads. You will also use some of your prep tools for painting. These tools will last for many years if conditioned, used, cleaned, and stored properly.

Brushes

You need three basic brushes.
- A 1½- to 2½-inch angular sash brush to paint woodwork and windows
- A 2-inch trim brush to cut in (paint a straight edge) at corners and ceiling lines and to paint woodwork
- A 3-inch flat brush to paint flat surfaces

There are two types of brushes: synthetic bristle and natural bristle (made with boar bristles). Synthetic bristle brushes work well with all types of paint. Natural bristle brushes absorb water easily and become limp, so use them only with alkyd paints and

other finishes that clean up with paint thinner.

Always buy the best brushes you can afford. A quality brush balances well in your hand, holds more paint, and controls paint flow onto the surface. It has a sturdy hardwood handle, a metal-reinforced neck, and a tapered end so it makes an even line when pressed against a flat surface. Such a brush has thick, flexible bristles with flagged (split) ends. Fan out the bristles and check the flags. The more there are, the more paint the brush will hold. Lightly flex the brush—it should feel springy. Finally, grip the brush before you buy it. It should feel comfortable and not heavy; a too-heavy brush quickly tires your hand.

Condition new brushes by working petroleum jelly into the bristles and up into the brush's heel. Then wash the brush with soap and warm water, and rinse. This washing removes the petroleum jelly from the bristle ends but leaves some of it in the heel. There it keeps paint from working up into the compacted bristles where it would be impossible to get out. This simple conditioning step makes painting neater and cleanup easier, and it prolongs bristle life. If your brushes receive heavy use, recondition them occasionally.

Rollers

A roller with an extension pole provides a fast, easy way to paint walls and ceilings. Buy a quality roller with a sturdy steel frame; nylon bearings; and a 9-inch-wide wire sleeve, also called a cage. It should have sealed ends and a comfortable handle threaded to receive a 4-foot-long extension pole. Don't buy a cheap roller. If it turns too slowly, it smears the paint; if it turns too fast, it causes spattering. Consider it a part of your permanent paint tool collection and invest accordingly.

Roller Covers

Always use the correct roller cover for your paint: a synthetic cover for latex paints; wool, wool and nylon blends, or mohair for alkyd paints. Cover naps range from $\frac{1}{16}$ to $1\frac{1}{4}$ inches long. When choosing a roller cover, check the

Roller Naps

Finish Texture	Surface to Be Painted	Nap Size
Smooth	Walls, floors, finish work, cabinets	$\frac{3}{16}$", $\frac{1}{4}$"
Medium smooth	Walls	$\frac{3}{8}$", $\frac{1}{2}$"
Rough	Textured walls, light stucco walls, masonry floors	$\frac{3}{4}$", 1"
Extra rough	Brick, concrete block, masonry, stucco	$1\frac{1}{4}$"

Tools for rolling (top left): bucket and screen, tray, rollers, extension handle, roller covers; for cleanup (top right): cloths, roller cleaning kit, spinner, scraper, brush comb; for masking (bottom left): tape, paint shield; for brushing (bottom): brushes with nylon, foam, and boar bristles; and for special applications (bottom right): mitt, HVLP sprayer, pad applicator.

specifications on the package to see which type of paint and surface it is intended for. As a general rule, the smoother the surface, the shorter the nap. Typically, a $\frac{3}{8}$- to $\frac{3}{4}$-inch nap is for most interior paint jobs. It hides the small flaws found in most flat walls and ceilings and does a good job of applying glossy finishes to smooth surfaces. Use a $\frac{1}{16}$-inch nap roller or a foam roller for extremely smooth surfaces. Use thick-napped wool or mohair covers to apply flat paint to rough surfaces, such as unglazed bricks and concrete blocks. Again, buy quality. A cheap cover may leave splotches and lint.

Roller Trays and Paint Screens

Roller trays are popular because they can be set on a stepladder, but they need to be refilled frequently and sometimes don't provide enough friction for the roller. A paint screen, or grid, hung inside a 5-gallon bucket, is a faster, neater way to evenly load your roller. Whether metal or plastic, the screen should be the same width as your roller. Dip the roller into the paint and run it over the screen to work the paint into the nap. If you use a tray, buy one with legs so it sits firmly on the shelf of a stepladder; that's its main advantage. A paint screen can be used in a paint tray, too.

Pad Applicators

Most pads have a synthetic nap bonded to a foam core. Their flat surface makes them suitable for a wide variety of jobs, especially cutting in, or

edging and painting flat trim. Some have threaded handles to accommodate an extension pole. Some have guide wheels so you make a perfect edge. Their advantages? Pads apply paint faster than brushes and leave less surface texture than rollers. They spatter and drip less, and most are disposable so they can be thrown away when the job is done. They work with either latex or alkyd paints. Their chief disadvantage? You must apply the paint with a single stroke; you can't spread paint or touch up missed spots by rubbing the pad back and forth.

Other Painting Tools

These are the most useful specialty paint applicators.

•Narrow trim rollers for woodwork, window sashes, and cabinets. Available in both napped and foam covers.

•A beveled roller for cutting in corners and ceiling lines, for painting borders, and for painting grooves in vertical paneling.

•A grooved-foam roller for painting spray-textured acoustical ceilings.

•A painter's mitt to paint pipes and contoured surfaces.

•A paint shield to protect adjacent surfaces when painting woodwork.

•A high-volume, low-pressure paint sprayer for painting irregular surfaces, such as louvered doors, panels, and wrought-iron trim.

•A paint edger, whose guide wheels eliminate the need to mask an adjacent surface. An edger works well only if surfaces are level, plumb, or square.

BASIC PAINTING TECHNIQUES

Painting is an easy skill to learn. Many techniques, such as holding a brush, come quite naturally. The trick is to learn the professional techniques that help you get paint on the wall quickly and create a flawless finish. These techniques are presented in this section by skills and by project.

Preparing the Paint

If you start work soon after you purchased your paint, it needs only a light stirring. For a single can, pour off the thin paint at the top of the can. Stir the thick paint in the bottom, then pour the thin paint back in and stir. If you have several cans, the paint in them could vary slightly in color, especially if it was custom-mixed. To get a uniform color throughout your job, box the paint. Some paints may also require straining or thinning.

Boxing

Pour all the paint for the job into a 5-gallon pail or bucket. Stir it with a stick until it is thoroughly mixed and uniform in color. Boxing eliminates slight color variations among cans of paint. Drive small nail holes into the grooves in the can rims, then pour the boxed paint back into the cans. Trapped paint will drain through the holes into the can. Tightly seal the lids on all but the first can.

Straining

If the paint has separated, stir the thick paint up from the bottom of each can until it is as free of lumps as possible.

Then box it as described, pouring it through a cloth paint strainer into the pail. If the paint has a thick scum or skin, don't try to mix it back into the paint. Instead, remove the skin and set it aside. When it has dried, wrap it in newspaper and discard it. Box the paint as described, pouring it through a cloth paint strainer into the pail.

Thinning

If paint has been stored for some time, it may need to be thinned as well as stirred. Box the paint and, as you stir it, decide how much thinning, if any, the paint needs. To do this, make several test strokes with the boxed paint. If your brush leaves furrows or your roller nap pulls the paint away from the wall, it needs thinning. Add an ounce of water or paint thinner, as appropriate; stir thoroughly; and test again. Continue this process until the paint makes an even film on the wall. Don't over-thin. If you have thinned and the paint still does not flow or adhere properly, talk to your paint dealer. You may be using the wrong brush or roller cover, or your surface may not be clean.

Holding a Paintbrush

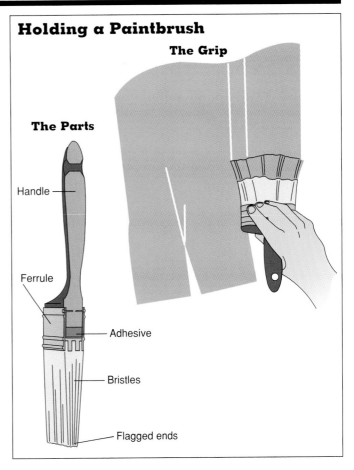

The Grip

The Parts

Handle

Ferrule

Adhesive

Bristles

Flagged ends

Painting With a Brush

Brushes are used for painting woodwork, cabinets, and rough-textured surfaces. They are also used to cut in the corners and edges of walls and ceilings, because a brush spreads paint efficiently and gives you more control. However, these advantages occur only when you use the correct brush for the job and hold it properly.

Use an angular sash brush to paint window sashes; use a trim brush or flat brush for cutting in. Don't use any brush that is wider than the surface being painted. A brush that is too wide tempts you to paint with its side, which splays its bristles and distorts its shape.

How to Hold a Paintbrush

Hold the brush lightly. Your thumb should support the underside of the brush while your fingers guide it from the top as you make your stroke. Note that the thumb and fingers rest against the brush's ferrule in this grip, not the handle. If it's more comfortable for you, you can hold a small trim brush like a pencil. In both grips, the handle rests in the crook of your thumb. However, if your hands are small or your brush is wide, wrap your fingers around the handle as you would a tennis racket. Shift your grip occasionally to avoid hand and arm fatigue.

Using a Brush

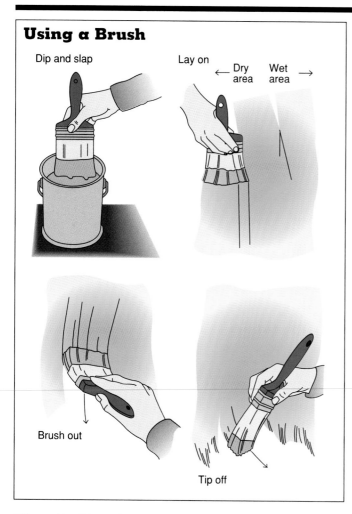

Dip and slap

Lay on

← Dry area

Wet area →

Brush out

Tip off

How to Brush On Paint

Paint walls and ceilings in 6-foot-wide sections. The paint for each section should slightly overlap that of the previous section. On walls and ceilings, use vertical strokes. On woodwork, paint with the grain.

The way you load and stroke a paintbrush, plus the speed and pressure with which you apply the stroke, affect the quality of a paint job. A paint stroke should consist of four movements.

Load the Brush

Dip one-third of the bristle length straight down into the paint. Lift the brush straight up and slap it lightly against the inside of the pail or can to remove excess paint. Don't drag the brush across the rim. This causes bristles to wear and clump, and it floods the rim with excess paint.

Lay On the Paint

Hold the brush at a 45-degree angle to the surface. Apply the paint in a long, even stroke, slightly overlapping the end of the previous stroke. The entire tip of the brush should touch the surface as you move along.

Brush Out the Paint

Now spread the paint evenly over the area. Use long, even strokes as you pull it from the painted into the unpainted area. Apply just enough pressure to flex the bristles and distribute the paint.

Tip Off the Paint

As you end the stroke, feather the paint edges with the tips of the bristles. To do this, lift the brush away from the wall while still moving through the stroke. This makes the paint film as thin as possible on the wet edge of the surface, which helps the paint blend in with the first paint stroke applied to the next section.

Painting With a Roller

Rollers spread paint quickly and easily. This makes them the preferred tool for painting large, flat spaces. However, they use more paint and are not as effective as brushes at covering irregular surfaces. Start by thoroughly wetting the roller cover, using water for latex paint and mineral spirits for alkyd paint, then run it over a clean towel until dry. This wetting-drying process removes lint and primes the roller to receive paint.

How to Load a Roller

Fill the paint tray or bucket with paint. Dip the roller fully into the paint. Lift it from the paint. Roll it over the raised pattern of the tray or the paint screen to work the paint into the nap. The roller should be full but not dripping when removed from the tray or bucket.

Roller Strokes

The most workable approach is to paint in 6-foot-wide sections. Do walls from baseboard to ceiling; do ceilings from wall to wall across the width, not the length. Each section needs to slightly overlap the section just painted. Do this by moving the roller over the surface in a series of overlapping M's. As you work, use medium pressure and move the roller slowly and smoothly over the wall. This will cut down on spattering and ensure even coverage.

First Stroke

Start at the baseboard on the left-hand edge of the section. Standing directly in front of your work, run the roller up to the ceiling in one long, steady stroke. This single pass helps prevent drips.

Remaining Strokes

Immediately pull the roller down at an angle and back up to make the center of the M. Then pull the roller down from ceiling to baseboard to complete the letter. Working left to right, continue making these bold, overlapping M strokes until you reach the right-hand edge of the section. Go back over the section with overlapping M's, working from right to left. (Work in reverse order if you are left-handed.) When you reach the left-hand edge of the section, it should be filled in with paint. Reload your roller 3 or 4 times during this entire process.

Laying-Off Strokes

The last step is to give the section a uniform appearance by finishing with a series of light

Using a Roller

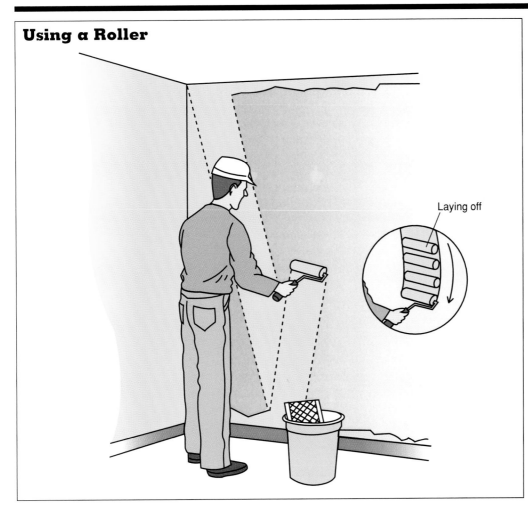

Laying off

strokes that smooth the paint in one direction, from top to bottom. To do this, lightly pull the roller down from the top of the wall to the baseboard. Lift the roller as you reach the end of the stroke. Return to the top and, overlapping the previous section by 1 inch, pull the roller down the wall again. Repeat this process until the entire section is smoothed.

Painting With a Pad

You cannot pull a pad back and forth over the paint in the same way you work a brush or roller. This makes it difficult to feather edges, so you run a greater chance of getting lap marks. If you use a pad, follow these steps.

1. Lightly moisten the pad with water or thinner, as appropriate. Towel-dry as you would a roller cover.

2. Dip the spreader into the paint. Take care not to soak the foam backing of the pad. Lift the spreader straight up and lightly rub it against the edge of the paint tray to remove any excess paint.

3. For painting trim or cutting in, use long, straight strokes, all in the same direction. For painting large, flat areas, apply the paint in a

thatching pattern—a combination of overlapping horizontal and vertical strokes, making each stroke just once. If the paint gushes out or runs, the pad is overloaded.

4. Feather the edges by gradually decreasing pressure as you reach the end of a section.

5. To finish, or lay off, run the almost-dry pad lightly over the freshly painted area, in one direction, top to bottom.

Painting With a Spray Gun

Modern high-volume, low-pressure (HVLP) sprayers eliminate the problem once characteristic of all paint

sprayers: overspraying. Unlike airless or air compressor sprayers, which use pressures of 2,500 psi or higher, HVLP sprayers use a pressure of 4 psi to propel paint onto a surface. This gives you incredible control compared to the conventional systems, which are better suited to exterior painting. HVLP sprayers are suitable for outdoor use, too, but they are of particular benefit indoors. They produce fine finishes on small interior surfaces, such as woodwork and cabinets. They lay down an even coat and get paint into areas you can't reach with a brush or roller. However, to provide these advantages, spray guns must be used properly. Follow these steps.

1. First, following the paint manufacturer's directions, thin the paint so it will atomize well. Use the appropriate thinner: water with latex paint, paint thinner with alkyd paint. If the paint manufacturer does not give directions for thinning the paint, follow the directions and testing methods presented in the manual provided by the sprayer manufacturer. To prevent clogging, pour the paint through a cloth paint strainer after it is thinned. Fill the sprayer's paint container.

2. Adjust the sprayer pattern to the shape best suited to the shape and width of the surface to be painted.

3. If spraying with an HVLP sprayer is new or unfamiliar to you, practice on a scrap of wood or cardboard. The paint should come out in an even pattern, without spattering. If it is coming out too

Using a Spray Gun

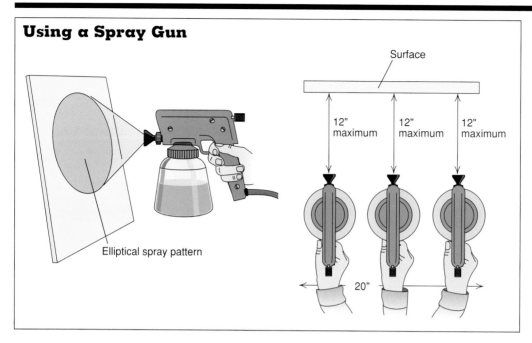

Elliptical spray pattern

Surface

12" maximum   12" maximum   12" maximum

20"

quickly or too slowly or if the pattern is the wrong size or shape, adjust the sprayer according to the manufacturer's directions.

4. All sprayers produce some overspray, so mask and drape surrounding surfaces you do not want spattered.

5. Hold the gun parallel to the floor, perpendicular to the surface to be sprayed, and 1 to 12 inches from it. The exact distance depends on the size of spray pattern you want—the farther you are from the surface, the larger the sprayed area. For best results, make 20-inch-long passes. Spray parallel to the surface with smooth passes at a consistent speed. Hold your hand and wrist so the sprayer stays parallel to the floor and the same distance from the surface throughout the pass. Otherwise you'll get an elliptical pattern that covers unevenly. Always press the trigger after the pass has begun and stop it before the pass is

complete. This, plus holding the sprayer equidistant from the surface throughout the pass, prevents paint buildup (especially along edges) and running or sagging paint.

6. Always make the first coat a thin coat. Allow it to dry completely before applying the second coat. Overlap passes slightly to get a consistent, professional finish.

7. If the sprayer clogs during spraying, shut it off, disconnect the cord, and unclog the nozzle according to the manufacturer's directions.

Paint Sprayer Safety

Read all instructions and safety precautions in the owner's manual before you use your sprayer. Here are the most important safety rules.

1. Use a respirator when you spray materials that contain harmful vapors.

2. Provide adequate exhaust and fresh air in the area being painted.

3. Keep the turbine as far as possible from the area being sprayed.

4. Plug the turbine into a grounded circuit only.

5. Don't smoke while spraying, and never operate the sprayer anywhere near an open flame.

6. Never try to clear the tip or otherwise adjust the sprayer while it is running.

7. Never point the sprayer at anyone, including yourself.

Painting With Aerosol Paints

Aerosol paints offer a quick, convenient, and easy way to paint a variety of surfaces. They are especially useful for small items and hard-to-reach places that are difficult to paint with a brush or roller. Aerosol paints have other advantages: They don't require auxiliary equipment, they make little mess, and they produce an excellent finish if applied correctly.

Apply these paints with the same spraying technique used with a power spray gun, following the safety precautions. Store aerosol paints as you would any other paint product. Before you start spraying, shake the container for a minute to thoroughly mix the paint. As you spray, press the valve all the way down and move the can evenly over the surface in a follow-through motion. Don't press the valve down until you have started the pass, and release it before you end the pass. Holding it longer produces drips and runs. Make no pass longer than 20 inches.

To prevent the nozzle's becoming clogged, rotate the valve a quarter turn after each pass. If it does become clogged, turn the can upside down and spray for a few seconds to clear it. If this doesn't work, pull the valve from the can and run your fingernail through the slit in its base. Replace the valve with a gentle twisting motion. Never stick pins or other sharp objects into the opening in the top of the can.

After painting, turn the can upside down and spray for a few seconds to clear the nozzle. Do the same before you dispose of used aerosol containers, keeping pressure on the valve until the hissing stops. This silence means the paint residue and propellant are spent. Never throw away an aerosol can until it is emptied of both product and propellant; otherwise it may explode if exposed to heat or fire in the trash dump. Never puncture an aerosol can—this also could cause an explosion.

HOW TO PAINT A ROOM

If you paint a room in the sequence presented in this chapter, paint on one surface will dry before adjacent surfaces are painted. And cleanup will be easy because you'll work gradually toward the floor. Ideally, two people paint a room together: One cuts in with a brush while the other follows with a roller.

Preparing the Room for Painting

You did much of the preparation required for painting when you set up the room for repairs and cleaning (see page 22). All you need do now is cover any exposed surfaces you want to protect from spatters, drips, and spills. This requires you to mask and drape the room. These two tasks prevent mistakes from causing damage and take the work out of cleanup.

Draping Walls

This essential step protects walls and woodwork from spatters while you paint the ceiling. Follow these steps.

1. Press the top half of 1½-inch-wide blue masking tape along the top of the walls. The tape's top edge should abut the ceiling.

2. Push plastic sheeting under the loose edge of the tape and press the tape down onto the plastic. The sheeting should drape down over the walls and baseboards.

3. Wait to remove the tape and sheeting until the paint on the ceiling is dry to the touch, so it won't pull off.

Masking Woodwork

This practical step protects your woodwork, whether bare or finished, from splotches and spatters as you cut in around it and paint the walls.

1. Use 1½-inch-wide blue masking tape or painting tape (a tape designed to prevent undertape seepage) for this job. Apply the tape along the side edge of window and door trims. The stuck edge should abut the wall. Leave the outside edge loose.

2. Press down the inside edge of the tape so paint can't seep under it.

3. If your project includes painting windows, now is the time to mask the glazing. You will put blue masking tape along the edges of all sections of glass, leaving a hairline crack of exposed glass between it and the window framing. Mask the top of the glass first; then one side; then the bottom edge; and, finally, the second side. This sequence makes it easy to remove the tape. Overlap the ends and press down on the tape to prevent paint from seeping under it. Wait to remove the tape until the paint is dry to the touch, so it won't run or pull away.

Draping Walls

1½" blue masking tape

Plastic sheeting

Masking Woodwork and Window Glass

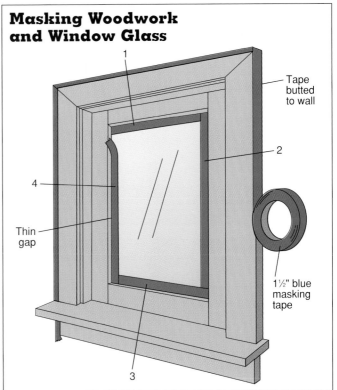

1

Tape butted to wall

2

4

Thin gap

3

1½" blue masking tape

Painting the Ceiling

To paint a ceiling, use a trim brush and a 9-inch-wide roller. The roller cover should have a ⅜-inch nap if the ceiling is smooth, a ½-inch to ¾-inch nap if it is textured. Attach a 4-foot extension to the roller handle so you can paint from the floor, or rig a scaffold as described in the section on ladders, page 23. Wear goggles and a scarf or cap in addition to other protective clothing.

Plan to finish the entire ceiling in one painting session. Allowing sections to dry at different times produces visible lap marks, the sign of a poor paint job. To avoid such flaws, always start a new section by overlapping the wet edge of the section you just painted. Also, always leave a wet edge for the next section by feathering or laying off your strokes.

Start in the corner farthest from the room's entry door. Visually divide the ceiling into 6-foot-wide sections. Paint one section at a time, working in rows across the width of the room and toward the entry wall. Apply the paint by cutting in and rolling, as described next. Repeat these techniques, section by section, until the ceiling is done.

Cutting In

Using your trim brush, apply the paint in a 4-inch-wide band on the ceiling along the wall-ceiling line, and around any obstructions, such as light fixtures. Flex the bristles just enough to make them fan out and create a straight edge. If working alone, cut in about 6 feet at a time so you maintain a wet edge for painting sections with the roller, then alternate between cutting in and rolling.

Rolling the Ceiling

With the roller, immediately cover the section by using the *M* pattern, blending the paint into the brush strokes at the perimeter. For a smooth finish, feather off the section by working the roller toward the entry wall. Remember to lift the roller before completing the stroke.

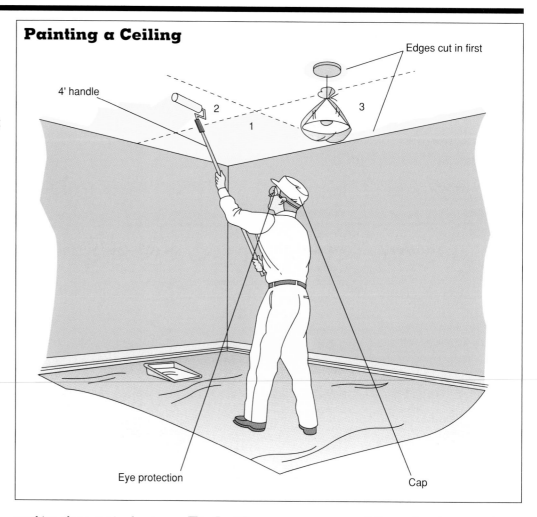

Painting a Ceiling

Edges cut in first

4' handle

2

1

3

Eye protection

Cap

Painting the Walls

Paint the walls with a trim brush or flat brush, whichever is easier to handle, and a 9-inch-wide roller. Use a cover with a ⅜-inch nap on smooth walls, ½-inch or ¾-inch nap on textured walls. A 4-foot extension pole makes the job easier.

Paint the walls when the ceiling is dry to the touch. Start in the same corner as the ceiling, and visually divide the wall into 6-foot-wide, 8-foot-high sections. Plan to complete each wall in one session so the sections don't dry at different times and leave lap marks. Each wall can dry at a different time, however. Apply the paint by cutting in and rolling, section by section, as described next.

Cutting In

Start in your original corner. Cut in a 4-inch-wide band of paint on the wall at the ceiling line, flexing the brush lightly so the bristles fan out and create a straight line. Then cut in the corner, along the baseboard, and around any openings in that section. If you are working alone, cut in 6 feet at a time so you maintain a wet edge.

Rolling the Walls

Immediately roll paint on the wall in *M*'s, blending into the cut-in paint. Use smooth, even strokes. Remember to lay off in one direction, as described for ceilings.

Painting Woodwork

The order for painting woodwork is this: window sashes, doors, door and window trim, wall paneling (if any), cabinets and bookshelves, moldings other than baseboards, and baseboards.

Window Sashes

Start early in the day so the windows will be dry enough to close at night. Remove all window hardware and open the windows. Follow the inside-out rule: First paint the wood nearest the glass, including the muntins; then work outward to the jambs (but paint the jambs later). Use your angular sash brush and paint with the grain—horizontal members with horizontal strokes, vertical members with vertical strokes from the top down. The order in which you paint the parts of the window depends on the window's style.

Double-hung Windows

Raise the lower sash to within 2 inches of the top of the window, and lower the upper sash to within 2 inches of the sill. Starting with the upper sash, paint as much of each sash as you can reach, working from the glass outward. Do not paint the bottom or underside edge of the upper sash's bottom rail; it should

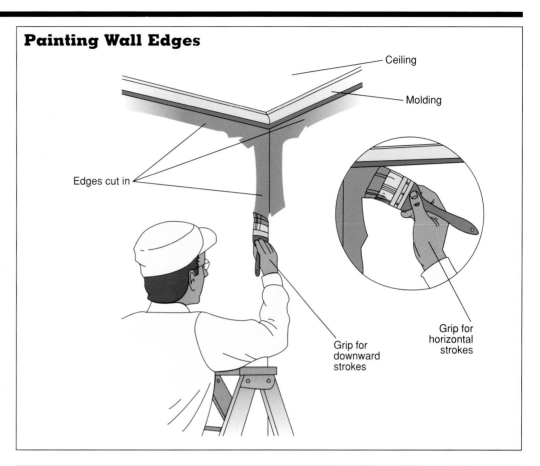

Painting Wall Edges

Ceiling

Molding

Edges cut in

Grip for horizontal strokes

Grip for downward strokes

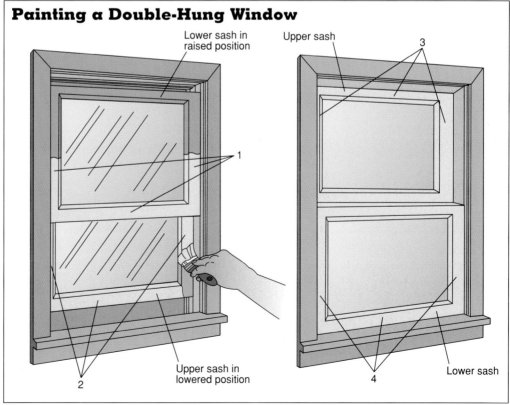

Painting a Double-Hung Window

Lower sash in raised position

Upper sash

3

1

2

Upper sash in lowered position

4

Lower sash

match the exterior paint. Do not paint the sash tracks. Don't paint the window jambs, stops, or casings (the trim around the windows) at this time. Slide the sashes back to within 2 inches of their normal closed positions—do not wait for them to dry. Starting with the lower sash, paint the remaining surfaces of each. Leave the sashes slightly open. Move them up and down several times while they are drying, to prevent sticking. When they are completely dry, use a razor blade to remove paint smears from the glass.

Casement, Awning, and Slider Windows

These windows are much easier to paint than double-hung windows. Open casement and awning windows slightly. Lift the moving halves of slider windows out of their track. Paint the muntins and sashes first, the hinge edge last. The latch edge, top, and bottom should be painted with exterior trim paint. Leave open to dry. When the paint is completely dry, use a razor blade to remove paint smears from the glass.

Doors

Remove all hardware and, if possible, remove the door. Painting a door that is lying flat is much easier than painting one that is hanging vertically in its frame. To remove a door, start with the bottom hinge. Drive the pin out by inserting, from beneath, a 16-penny (16d) nail into the hole in the hinge knuckles and tapping it with a hammer, or drive the knob of the hinge

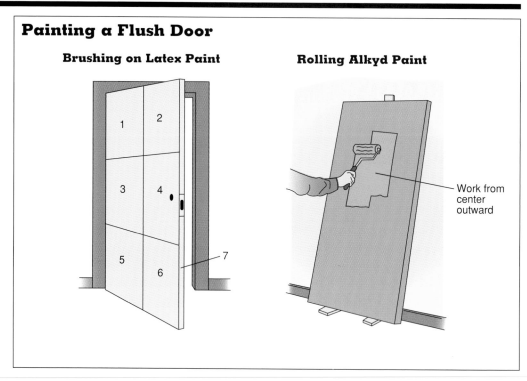

Painting a Flush Door

Brushing on Latex Paint

Rolling Alkyd Paint

Work from center outward

pin upward with a hammer and screwdriver or chisel. (Never remove the top hinge first; the door's weight could break the bottom hinge.) While someone holds the door, drive out the top pin. Lift the door off its hinges and lay it across 2 sawhorses, or prop it against a wall. If you leave it in its frame, wedge it open with a block of wood.

If you are using latex paint, paint the door with a flat brush. Use a roller to apply alkyd paint, then spread and smooth it with a trim brush. If you paint only one side of a door, paint the latch edge to match the room into which it opens. The hinge edge should match the room it opens away from. Quickly wipe up any paint that runs onto the reverse side of the door. Paint in sections as dictated by the door's style. However, complete the job in one session.

Flush Doors

If you are applying latex paint, coat the top third of the door, working from left to right and brushing from the top down (with the grain); then the middle third; and finally the bottom third. Always maintain a fully loaded brush, and paint from wet into dry areas, feathering your final strokes. After coating the door's face, paint its latch edge, but don't paint the jamb at this time. Paint the hinge edge only if appropriate.

If you are using alkyd paint, apply it with a roller, working outward from the center, first up and then down. Immediately after rolling, use a trim brush to spread and even out the paint. Brush from the top down. Then paint the latch edge. Paint the hinge edge only if appropriate.

Paneled Doors

Paint with a flat brush. Brushing with the grain, paint the panels first, in this order: panel moldings, panel recesses, panel fronts. Next paint the frame's central vertical sections. Paint the horizontal sections, followed by the outer vertical sections. Then paint the latch edge, but don't paint the jamb at this time. Paint the hinge edge only if appropriate.

Door and Window Trim

Again, remember to paint with the grain, horizontal sections with horizontal strokes, vertical sections with vertical strokes, working from the top down. First, use a sash brush to paint the edges of trim nearest the wall. Use masking tape, painting tape (special tape with a micro-barrier edge, not to be confused with blue masking tape), or a paint

Painting a Paneled Door

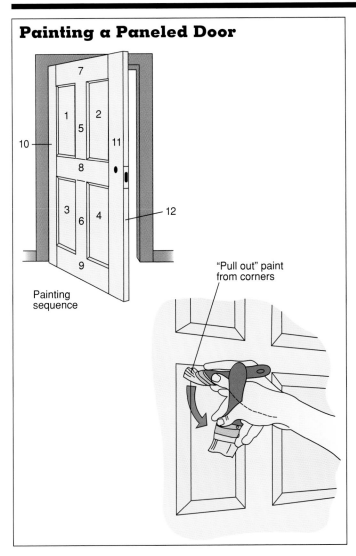

Painting
sequence

"Pull out" paint
from corners

Painting Door Trim

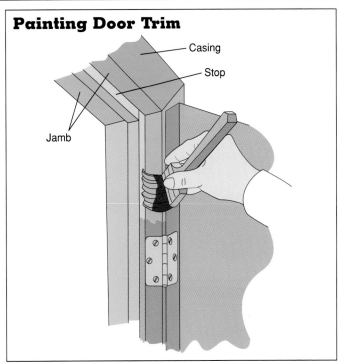

Casing

Stop

Jamb

Painting a Cabinet

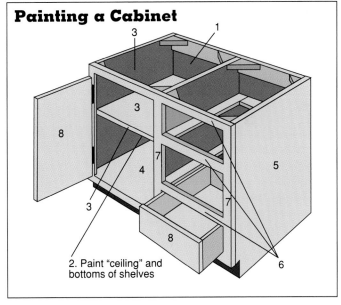

2. Paint "ceiling" and
bottoms of shelves

shield to protect the adjacent wall. Then follow these steps.

For windows, open the window slightly. First, paint the jamb and stops. Then paint the face trim in this order: head casing, side casings, and bottom casing (on casements and sliders) or stool and apron (on double-hung windows). Let dry. Move double-hung windows several times during the drying period to prevent sticking.

For doors, first paint the jamb and the edge of the stop facing the door. Next paint the head casing, then the side casings. Of course, paint the entire jamb, stop and all, if the door is to be the same color on both sides.

Wall Paneling

Paint the same as paneled doors, working from recessed panels outward toward the panel frames and trim.

Cabinets and Bookshelves

Remove all hardware. Then remove the drawers, adjustable shelves, and, if possible, doors. Set them aside. Paint all vertical surfaces from the top down; all horizontal surfaces with lateral strokes. Paint in this order.

1. The back wall

2. The inside "ceiling," followed by the underside of fixed shelves

3. The side walls, followed by the top and leading edge of fixed shelves

4. The inside floor, or the bottom

5. The exposed sides, if any

6. The horizontal members of the face frame

7. The vertical members of the face frame

Painting Louvered Shutters

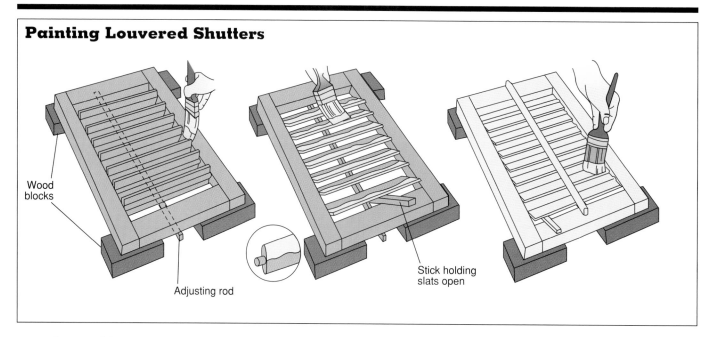

Wood blocks

Adjusting rod

Stick holding slats open

8. All areas of doors, and drawer fronts

9. The underside of the exterior, if exposed.

Adjustable Shelves, Doors, and Drawer Fronts

Shelves and doors are easier to paint if they are removed and laid flat. Start with the shelves and paint in the following order, letting each surface dry completely before painting the next.

1. The underside and back edge of adjustable shelves

2. The top and leading edge of the shelves

3. The interior side of the doors

4. The door fronts and leading edges

5. The drawer fronts and leading edges, with drawer stood up on its back. Do not paint any other part of the drawer or the drawer openings inside the cabinet.

Moldings and Baseboards

Work from the top down, painting in this order: ceiling moldings, picture moldings, chair rails, and baseboards. Paint standard-width moldings with a trim brush, narrow moldings with a sash brush, wide moldings with a flat brush. Use a paint shield, masking tape, or painting tape to protect surrounding surfaces from paint. Use the following technique to apply paint.

1. Paint the top edge of the molding first. The paint should cover any caulk.

2. Paint the bottom edge. Use the paint shield to pull the carpet nap away from the baseboards.

3. Fill in between the 2 edges, finishing with light brush strokes to create a smooth surface. If you are painting wide trim with alkyd paint, you can, if you wish, roll the paint between the top and bottom edges and then brush it smooth.

Interior Shutters

There are two types of shutters: paneled and louvered. To paint either type, remove the hardware first, then remove the shutters from the window. Lay them on sawhorses or blocks of wood, backside up, and paint with a brush, as described next, or with a spray gun or aerosol paint, as described on pages 45 and 46.

Paneled Shutters

Paint paneled shutters the same way you paint paneled doors, except paint both sides and all edges. Or you can paint with a spray gun or aerosol paint.

Louvered Shutters

Movable louvers can be tedious to paint. The easiest way is with a spray gun or aerosol paint. If you don't have access to either or wish to paint by hand, use a trim brush and work in this order.

1. Set the louvers so they are fully open. Paint the inside edges of the frame. Then paint the inside edge of the adjusting rod. Let dry.

2. Insert a stick between the frame and the top louver to keep the slats open while you paint. Start with the top louver and paint both the front and the back of the top half of each slat, working from the end of each slat toward the center. Let dry.

3. Turn the shutter over and paint the rest of the adjusting rod and the bottom half of the louvers. Let dry.

4. Paint the frame and its outer edges. First paint the horizontal sections with horizontal strokes, then vertical sections with vertical strokes from the top down. Let dry.

5. Turn the shutter over and paint the backside of the frame the same way. Let dry and rehang.

Special Situations

Certain painting details, such as borders or texture patterns, and some surfaces, such as masonry, call for special painting techniques.

Painting Borders

Start by painting the wall or ceiling its main color. Then decide where you want the border to go and how wide you want it to be. When the base paint has dried thoroughly, snap white chalk lines to mark both edges of the border. Apply painting tape along these chalk lines, pressing the sticky edge in place. Don't use regular masking tape—paint may ooze under it. When the tape is in place, use a brush, roller, or pad to paint the border the appropriate color. Apply 2 coats of paint if necessary to mask the base color. Remove the tape when the paint is dry.

Applying Textured Paints

Textured paints are thick-bodied paints that put a coarse decorative texture on a wall, hide small flaws, and help smooth uneven walls. They're easy to apply. Simply roll on the paint and work it into a textured pattern with a tool.

Textured paint comes as a premixed latex paint or as a dry powder. The premixed latex paint has medium body, stiff enough for light stippled textures. The dry powder, which comes in 25-pound bags, is more versatile. Mix it with water until you get the stiffness you need to make the desired pattern. Mix small quantities and practice different textures on a sample board, using a roller to apply the paint and then the tool you've chosen to produce the pattern. Once you find a pattern you like, practice it until you master the strokes. Try one of these common patterns.

A sponge creates a pattern on fresh textured paint. See page 54 for pattern instructions.

The stippled pattern is created by a roller (top), the swirls by a whisk broom (bottom).

Top left: For a trowel pattern, use a traditional plaster trowel or a taping knife to flatten a textured surface.
Bottom: A rag creates random peaks and ridges in textured paint.
Top right: A dry brush pats textured paint onto a wall in varied patterns.

Stipple Pattern

Use a 1¼-inch nap roller cover or a texture roller cover. Roll it through the paint in smoothing strokes similar to those used to lay off paint. This produces an even, overall pattern similar to that of a sprayed textured ceiling. In fact, you can use this pattern to repair small areas in a textured ceiling. Vary the pressure and direction of your strokes to make a random pattern.

Sponged Pattern

Randomly dab, drag, or swirl a natural sponge over the surface to create a pattern. Choose a sponge with medium-sized holes. Occasionally change the direction in which you move the sponge to avoid creating a regular pattern.

Swirl Pattern

Use a whisk broom or wallpaper brush to sweep semi-circular loops across the surface. Overlap the loops as you go.

Trowel Pattern

Apply textured paint in one of the patterns described and let it get almost dry. Then trowel over the paint to knock off the peaks and partially smooth out the texture.

Rag Pattern

Apply texture with a crumpled rag. To achieve different effects, vary the amount of texture paint on the rag, the amount of pressure applying it to the wall, and the direction in which you hold your hand as you press the rag to the wall.

Brush Pattern

Use the flat side of a dry paint brush to dab texture paint onto the wall. Use a quick, short, patting motion, varying the direction of the brush to create ridges and patterns.

Painting Masonry

To paint masonry you need special materials and techniques because of alkali deposits; water seepage; and the coarse, porous texture. Efflorescence—a white, powdery alkali deposit found on masonry surfaces—is produced when moisture migrates through concrete and mortar as a result of leaks or, in the case of new work, normal hydration. If you plan to paint new masonry, wait at least six months for the concrete or mortar to cure, then paint. If you plan to paint old masonry, repair any active leaks and clean the alkali off the surface before painting.

Filling Cracks and Holes

Latex masonry paints, which breathe and are more suitable for masonry than alkyd paints, are thick enough to fill small flaws such as hairline cracks; larger flaws, common in brick and concrete block walls, require repair. Dig out any loose material, dust the crack or hole with a clean brush, wet the area, and patch with cement or mortar. Wet the repaired area and let cure for 2 weeks.

Cleaning the Surface

Before cleaning any masonry surface, scrub it with a wire brush and a liquid laundry detergent. Use a mixture of muriatic acid and water to remove any alkali deposits. Wearing latex gloves and goggles, pour 1 quart muriatic acid into 3 quarts water. Always add acid to water, never the other way around. Using a scrub brush, wash the surface with the acid solution. Rins with water. Let dry.

Sealing

Coat the wall with penetrating sealer as soon as possible after the acid solution dries. This prevents the masonry from pulling more alkali to the surface. If the surface is too slick for a penetrating sealer, degloss it with the muriatic acid solution; apply it with a wire brush. If the surface is too porous, paint it with a masonry sealer designed to fill pores. Another sealer, known as a masonry surface conditioner, seals in and hardens unpainted masonry as well as masonry covered with aging paint. If it's covered with flaking paint, try scrubbing off the paint with liquid laundry detergent and a scrub brush, or strip it with the acid solution and a wire brush. If these steps don't work, hire a professional to sandblast the surface.

Painting

To apply paint to masonry, use a roller with a ¾-inch-nap cover or a large thick-bristled brush. These tools help the paint penetrate the rough texture. Most jobs require 2 coats, the sealer being the first.

Latex masonry paint is used to coat most masonry surfaces, including brick. However, there are many specialty masonry paints for surfaces such as floors and stairs. Check with your paint dealer.

Painting masonry, such as this interior brick wall, requires careful preparation to ensure that the paint will adhere properly.

APPLYING DECORATIVE PAINT FINISHES

Paints and enamels provide a solid, opaque coat of color. Nice, but plain. Decorative paint finishes, on the other hand, give walls rich texture, glowing color, and inviting style because they consist of colors layered over one another. They are also an easy and inexpensive way to satisfy an urge for creativity.

Five Decorative Paint Finishes

There are dozens of decorative paint finishes, ranging from simple stenciling to elaborate faux marble and trompe l'oeil. The latter look like something other than what they are—paint applied to a flat surface. Many are too difficult for anyone but a trained professional to do well, and many are too elaborate for most homes. However, four finishes—sponging, rag rolling, color washing, and stenciling—lie within the average person's ability. A fifth, dragging, is something you might try if you're adventurous.

The Basic Process

Decorative finishes are applied in two stages: an opaque base coat followed by several topcoats. The topcoats range from paint taken straight out of the can to transparent washes and glazes. They are applied in one of two ways: positive or negative. In a positive application, the colors and pattern go over the base coat. Sponging, rag rolling, color washing, and

stenciling are positive techniques. In a negative application, a glaze is brushed over the base coat and then some of it is removed before it dries. Dragging is a negative technique; sponging and rag rolling can also be done this way, by applying the topcoat with a roller and then sponging or ragging it off.

You can use either latex or alkyd interior paints to create decorative paint finishes. Latex paints work especially well for sponging and stenciling. They produce strong, clear patterns when used full strength. Thin them to a wash and they produce soft, mottled patterns. However, remember that latex paints dry quickly, which limits the time you have to work the pattern until harsh edges develop. Latex paints also give you the advantage of soap-and-water cleanup.

Alkyd paints work well for the five finishes described here, producing translucent colored films when thinned with oil glazes. They dry slowly, so you have time to work them until you get a soft edge. However, alkyd paints must be cleaned with mineral spirits or paint thinner.

Whichever decorative finish you choose, the base coat

Painting techniques such as glazing, ragging, and dry-brushing contribute to an aura of antiquity (top) and imbue two-toned stripes with subtle hints of European style (bottom).

and the topcoats must be the same type of paint. A latex base requires latex topcoats; an alkyd base coat requires alkyd topcoats. All base coats, latex or alkyd, should have an eggshell, or satin, finish. Make topcoats with flat or eggshell paints.

Washes and Glazes

Washes and glazes give decorative finishes their interesting texture and luminous color. Washes produce a crisp tex-ture; glazes produce a soft, blurry finish. Because you mix the topcoats yourself, you, and you alone, decide the color and the degree of translucency. To avoid mistakes and disappointments, practice your chosen technique on a sample board before you paint the room. Experiment with different formulas until you get an effect you like. Use the following formulas as a starting point for making the topcoats. Buy the ingredients at paint retailers or art supply stores.

Color Wash

A wash is a thinned latex paint. It can contain as much as 90 percent water. However, the more paint the wash contains, the more opaque and durable the finish. Start with a ratio of 1 part latex paint to 2 parts water. Add more water in small amounts until you get the translucency you desire. A clear acrylic latex urethane finish also makes a good latex color wash. Tint it to the color you desire with colorants.

Alkyd Glaze

An alkyd glaze is alkyd paint thinned with a commercial oil glaze (or commercial glazing liquid) and a paint thinner. Start by mixing equal parts of these 3 ingredients. This produces a moderately translucent glaze suitable for rag rolling and sponging. For greater translucency, combine 5 parts commercial oil glaze with 1 part each alkyd paint and paint thinner. You can add a little linseed oil to slow drying time if desired. This

A light wash gives these walls an almost translucent softness.

Look closely at the plate and the wall alcove: They are painted onto the wall. This ultra-realistic style of rendering is known as trompe l'oeil ("fool the eye").

glaze is excellent for color-washing walls.

Sponging

Sponging is the quickest, easiest way to put layers of color on walls and other flat surfaces. It is an ideal finish for a beginner to apply. You simply dip a natural sea sponge in paint and dab it on the wall in a random pattern. Do this with several colors, each applied in its own layer. The colors merge to create a dappled effect. Sponged patterns range from soft, light, and airy to distinct, dense, and complex. They are suitable to all informal settings, from contemporary to country.

The finished appearance depends on the colors. Obviously, you can sponge dark colors over a light base, or light colors over a dark base, or anything else you want. However, tone-on-tone pastels

or neutrals, which produce the subtle, cloudy effect characteristic of sponging, work best for beginners. Use two topcoat colors in addition to the base coat, all from the same color family. The base coat can be several tones lighter than the lightest topcoat. Choose colors that are one to three tones apart in the manufacturer's color chip system (or tell the paint dealer you want ⅛-tone color breaks). For example, use a pale yellow as the base coat and use a medium and a light yellow as the topcoats.

The Sponge

Use a natural sea sponge with medium-sized holes. Small holes create a spotty effect, large holes a coarse one. Prime the sponge by soaking it in water and wringing it out until it's damp—this will keep the sponge pliable and prevent it from thinning the paint.

The Stroke

Wear latex gloves. Apply the paint with a pounce stroke. This is a dabbing or tapping motion, straight at the wall, that does not twist or roll the sponge on the wall. Make the movements quickly and

in random directions. They should cover the wall evenly. To avoid making a regular or identifiable pattern, vary the way you hold your hand and occasionally turn the sponge clockwise.

This sponge pattern consists of three layers of paint: a base coat of pale yellow, a sponge coat of a darker shade of yellow-orange, and a final sponge coat of green.

Sponging

1. Dip damp sponge

First topcoat

2. Remove excess paint

3. Dab color onto wall

Wall painted with base coat

4. After drying, repeat with second topcoat

5. Apply final wash or glaze

The Technique

A topcoat can be full-strength paint, a wash, or a glaze. Washes create a pale, muted effect. Glazes create a soft, glowing effect.

1. Paint the walls the base color. Let dry overnight.

2. Pour the first topcoat into a tray (lining the tray with aluminum foil will speed cleanup). Dip the damp sponge into the paint. Dab it on a piece of clean cardboard to remove the excess. Start in a corner at the top of the wall. Using a gentle pounce stroke, paint in a random pattern. Let plenty of background show through with this first coat. Reload your sponge as often as necessary. In corners, use a small brush, or a sea sponge cut at a 90-degree angle.

3. Apply the second topcoat the same way, overlapping the first. The 2 colors should merge, but still let the base color show through. Let dry.

4. Dilute the base color until you get a very thin, translucent wash or glaze. With the sponge, dab it over the wall lightly, overlapping the topcoats and base coat. This creates a pleasing blend of colors.

Rag Rolling

Rag rolling is an easy technique for the beginner. It is similar to sponging, only you use clean rags to roll on the topcoats. It produces a sophisticated effect.

The finished appearance depends on the colors. Bold effects are created by contrasting colors; muted effects result from using only slightly differentiated colors. For the beginner, the best choice is two topcoat colors, using colors from the same color family to create tone-on-tone pastel or neutral color schemes. The base coat can be several tones lighter than the lightest topcoat. Then, just as with sponging, separate the topcoats from one another by one to three tones in the manufacturer's color chip system.

The Rags

You'll need clean, lint-free rags, such as cloth diapers or cheesecloth. Use the same

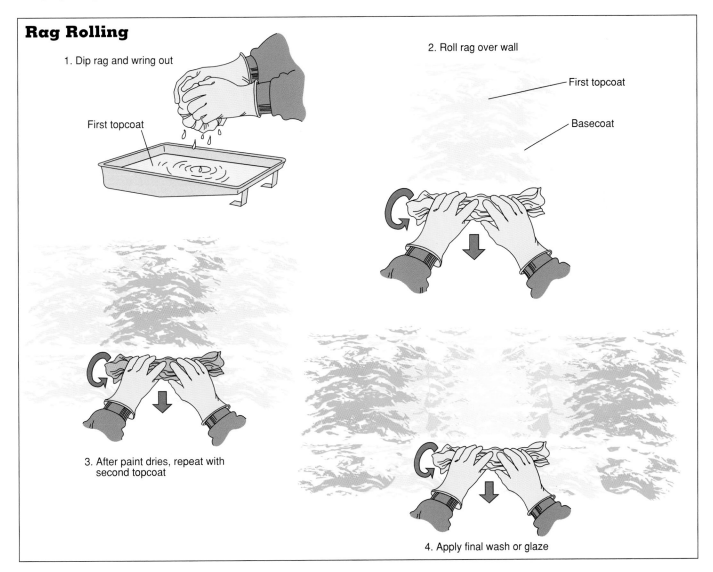

Rag Rolling

1. Dip rag and wring out

First topcoat

2. Roll rag over wall

First topcoat

Basecoat

3. After paint dries, repeat with second topcoat

4. Apply final wash or glaze

material throughout the job. Cut it into 1½- to 2-foot squares.

The Technique

To vary the effect, frequently change the pressure you use to roll the rags on the wall. Overlap the topcoats as you work. This blends the colors together and softens their edges, producing the sense of depth and glowing color characteristic of rag rolling. Change directions occasionally to create a pleasing effect. Above all, avoid any sense of a regular pattern.

1. Paint the walls the base color. Let dry overnight.

2. Pour the first topcoat color into a tray. Wear latex gloves. Dip the rag into the paint and wring it out slightly to remove excess paint. Then bunch or twist it into a roll. Start in a corner at the top of the wall. Slowly roll the rag downward over the base coat, letting plenty of background color show through this first topcoat. As often as necessary, change rags to prevent paint buildup. Let dry overnight.

3. Apply the second topcoat in the same way, overlapping the first topcoat color. The 2 colors should merge but allow the base color to show through.

4. Now dilute the base color until you get a very thin, translucent wash or glaze, and apply it in the same way.

Color Washing

This simple decorative finish produces walls with a soft, mellow, aged appearance. The technique involves building up a series of the thinnest possible layers of color. Apply each layer unevenly so the other colors show through. The result is a simple, unpretentious finish suitable for small rooms and country settings.

Use washes or glazes for the topcoats. Washes produce the powdered color effect reminiscent of old limewashed walls. Glazes produce a rich gloss finish with a warm, inner glow. Typically, two or three topcoats give the best results.

The Technique

Traditionally, color-washed walls have a white or off-white base coat covered with two or three topcoats of a very thin wash or glaze. Each topcoat is a different color, but each color can be from the same family, separated from one another by three or four adjacent tones, or you can use colors from closely related color families. For example, a white base coat with a blue cast could be topcoated with washes or glazes of red-purple, purple, and blue-purple; or try blue, blue green, and blue-purple.

1. Apply the base coat. Let dry overnight.

2. Apply the first topcoat with a flat (not tapered) brush. Move the brush in all directions, varying the size and shape of the fresh paint patches so a lot of the background color shows through. Avoid an even look, and brush or dab out any obvious or hard edges. Let dry overnight.

3. Apply the remaining topcoats the same way, overlapping the previous brush strokes. Let dry overnight.

4. Apply a clear finish coat of matte polyurethane for protection.

Stenciling

A well-known folk art, stenciling doesn't need much introduction. Most people know it as a simple and inexpensive craft. It is versatile also; stenciled designs enhance all types of interior settings. You can paint stencils on any clean, dry surface.

Use latex paints or artist's acrylics. Like latex paints, artist's acrylics are water-soluble, produce opaque colors, and dry quickly. You can buy them at art supply stores. Some artists stencil with latex washes, but this requires advanced skills. A beginner does best with a thick, pasty paint.

The Stencil

Stenciled designs range from simple one-color motifs to elaborate multilayered designs. The most effective stencil designs use no more than four colors, one of which is black. Each color requires a separate acetate stencil. You can use precut stencils in standard designs, available at art supply and craft stores, or you can cut your own.

To make your own stencil design, look for patterns or pattern ideas in folk art books, decorating books, and stencil pattern books at the library. You'll also find stencil pattern books in art supply stores. If you are ambitious and confident, draw your own design. Simple geometric or stylized designs work best, especially for beginners. The bridges (partitions between cutout areas in the stencil) should be wide enough to separate the painted areas effectively. If the bridges are too narrow—less

An alternative rag-rolling technique, shown here, is to brush on the top coat and then remove some of it with a rag before the paint dries. Work in small sections.

Stenciling

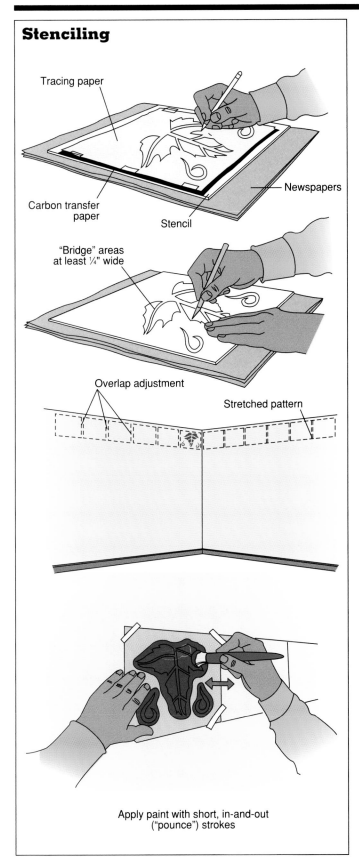

Tracing paper

Carbon transfer paper

Stencil

Newspapers

"Bridge" areas at least ¼" wide

Overlap adjustment

Stretched pattern

Apply paint with short, in-and-out ("pounce") strokes

than ¼ inch—the result is blobs of paint instead of a design. Narrow bridges also cause a stencil to break easily.

Trace the design, using carbon paper, or transfer it onto graph paper. If necessary, enlarge it with a photocopier. Then transfer it onto acetate with carbon paper and a pencil (remember, you need a separate stencil for each color). Do not cut a stencil out of cardboard. Its paper edges will fray and expand with repeated exposure to the paint, eventually distorting the design. Use a craft knife to carefully cut out the areas that will be painted. Mark each stencil so you can align the layers during painting.

The Stencil Stroke

Use a flat stencil brush to apply the paint through the cutout sections. Work the brush with a pounding or tapping movement, similar to pouncing, straight at the wall; do not rub against the edges of the cutout. Some stencil artists like to apply their paints more thinly in the center of large cutout sections, which keeps the design from becoming too dense, but this is a technique that requires practice and a fair degree of skill.

The Technique

Be sure to let each layer dry overnight before you apply the next layer.

1. Measure and mark the stencil locations, using a white chalk line, or steel tape measure and ruler. Adjust the space between the stencil positions for the best placement on the wall.

2. With regular masking tape or blue masking tape, anchor the first stencil in place at the starting point.

This pattern is being created with two stencils—one for the green leaves and one for the red rose.

3. Dip the stencil brush into the paint about one-third of its bristle length. Lift it out of the paint and tap it on a sheet of clean cardboard or paper to remove any excess paint. Too much paint will bleed under the stencil and ruin the design.

4. Holding the stencil in place with your free hand, pounce the paint over the cut-out area. Work from the edges toward the center.

5. Carefully lift the stencil and reposition it to make the next section of the design. Repeat the pouncing process until the first layer is complete throughout the room. Let dry overnight.

6. Repeat these steps for each additional layer until the entire design is complete.

7. Clean each stencil with soap and water as often as necessary to prevent smudges and smears. Dry thoroughly before using again.

8. If the design will receive wear, give it several coats of clear polyurethane finish for protection.

Dragging

Dragging requires a steady hand and cool nerves. It involves applying a glaze coat to a wall and then removing some of it before it dries. Only the most confident beginners should attempt dragging. The technique produces a finely striped effect called strié or combing. The resulting texture, barely visible from a few feet away, has a rich and glowing depth. The look is formal and elegant.

Alkyd paints provide the best medium for dragging: Latex paints dry too quickly. Use two colors from the same color family: a base coat and a topcoat that is as much as five tones darker. It can be a deeper tone than you actually want because the final effect will be lighter. Apply both coats with a roller.

The Removal Tool

Any number of tools can be used to pull off the glaze. Professional painters often use a rubber squeegee notched at $\frac{1}{4}$-, $\frac{1}{8}$-, or $\frac{1}{16}$-inch intervals. Quicker, simpler, and cheaper to use than a brush, it is also easier to control. Other options include a dragging brush or a wallpaper brush used as a dragging brush. *Note:* Because you are removing, not applying, color, you must clean the tool with paint thinner after completing each strip.

The Technique

Dragging is easier if you have a partner. One person applies the glaze while the other follows along and removes it. If you work alone, work in sections no more than 24 inches wide. Although this is a craft and your strokes don't have to be perfect, you do want to keep them as straight as possible, so snap white chalk lines to mark the sections. The best technique is to pull the dragging tool from the top to a point about two-thirds of the way down the wall, then complete the section, pulling from the baseboard up. Feather the strokes as the two sections meet, to avoid a heavy glaze buildup at the bottom of the wall. Be sure to vary the meeting line from section to section so you don't create a distinct seam around the room.

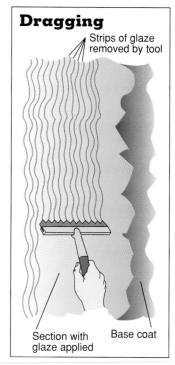

Dragging

Strips of glaze removed by tool

Section with glaze applied

Base coat

1. Apply the base coat. Let dry overnight.

2. Mix the glaze and pour it into a paint tray. Using a roller, apply the glaze to the first section, from baseboard to ceiling.

3. Immediately drag the removal tool down through the glaze from the ceiling, stopping two-thirds of the way to the baseboard. Make as straight a stroke as possible. Clean the removal tool and repeat the dragging stroke, overlapping the first stroke slightly. Complete until you are within one stroke of the wet edge, then finish the bottom strokes.

4. Roll on the next section of glaze, overlapping the first section slightly. Repeat the dragging process, but choose a different line for the meeting point of downward and upward strokes. Repeat these steps around the room.

Dragging a dry brush through wet paint produces this striated pattern.

CLEANUP AND STORAGE

Proper cleaning and storage of tools and paint containers will pay off. Quality tools, carefully maintained, will serve you well for a long time. Paint kept in airtight containers should last indefinitely.

Tool Cleanup

Most cleanup involves soaking, rinsing, and drying, but techniques vary by the type of tool being cleaned and the type of paint.

Brushes

1. Scrape off excess paint against the edge of a board.

2. If the paint is latex, wash the brush in warm, soapy water and rinse well. If the paint is alkyd, soak the brush in paint thinner or turpentine, then work the solvent through the bristles. Repeat with fresh solvent until the liquid remains clean. Shake the brush outdoors, using a sharp snapping motion to remove as much solvent as possible. If the bristles are synthetic, also wash them in warm, soapy water and rinse well.

3. Comb the bristles with a paintbrush comb. To dry the brush, twirl it inside a cardboard box or large pail, either by hand or with a paintbrush spinner.

4. Wrap the dry brush in its original cover or plain wrapping paper. Use a rubber band to hold the paper in place. Store the brush by laying it flat or hanging it by its handle.

5. Store the dirty solvent in a closed container, label it, let the solids settle, and reuse the liquid for subsequent cleanings until it gets sticky.

Rollers and Trays

1. Remove excess paint by scraping the roller head over the edge of the paint tray or bucket or by scraping it with the curved side of a cleaning tool or a piece of cardboard. Pour leftover paint into the paint can.

2. For latex paint, flush the roller assembly thoroughly under a strong stream of water. Remove the roller cover and wash it in warm, soapy water. Rinse with clear water. If alkyd, soak the cover in solvent. Wearing latex gloves, work the solvent into the nap and then rinse the cover with fresh solvent. Repeat soaking and rinsing until the solvent runs clear.

3. Squeeze excess water from the cover with your hands. Then roll the cover on a clean terry towel to remove moisture, or twirl it with a paintbrush spinner. Then stand it on end on a dry towel.

4. Clean the roller carriage and handle and the paint tray in the same way you cleaned the roller, disassembling parts as needed. Dry, reassemble, and hang for storage.

5. After the cover dries, wrap it in a clean towel or wrapping paper. Store it standing on its end so the nap doesn't flatten.

Other Tools

If you use paint pads that are disposable, let them dry completely and then toss them into the trash. Clean reusable pads the same way as roller covers. To clean a spray gun, follow the manufacturer's directions.

Personal Cleanup

Soap and water cleans up latex paint. However, be sure to launder clothes spattered with latex paint before it dries. Latex paint cleaners, available from paint dealers, will remove dried latex paint from shoes and similar surfaces.

Paint thinner cleans up alkyd paints but is very hard on skin. Try a mechanic's hand cleaner instead—it works for removing wet alkyd paint from clothing, also. Apply it, then immediately launder clothing. If you do use paint thinner to remove paint from your skin, dab it only on the paint spots, keep it away from your eyes, and immediately wash your skin with soap and water. Then dry your skin and rub lotion into it.

Storage of Leftover Paint Products

Store leftover paint products in tightly sealed cans, preferably the cans in which they came. Use wet paper towels to clean paint from the rim grooves, then seal the can. Store the can in a warm, dry place away from open flame. A lockable metal cabinet in a heated basement is ideal. Avoid porches, storage sheds, or other unconditioned spaces.

Dispose of small amounts of leftover paint by brushing it on cardboard. Let the cardboard dry and then throw it into the trash. If you have too much leftover paint to handle this way, try to give it to an organization that can use it (such as a local theater group, craft group, school, or charity). Otherwise, dispose of paint products as household hazardous wastes.

Disposal of Hazardous Paint Products

Most paint products are classed as household hazardous wastes. Do not dispose of these products, including latex paints, by pouring them down the drain, into a storm sewer, or onto the ground, and do not throw them into the trash. Take them to an authorized household hazardous waste disposal site. Your county's solid waste disposal office should be able to direct you. (Check the label of the paint product—for latex paint, you may be able to fill the can with cat litter or shredded newspaper and let it set up, then throw it in the trash.)

Wipe out empty cans and buckets with newspaper or paper towels. Let the containers dry, then throw them into the trash. Let paint-soiled newspapers, paper towels, rags, and plastic sheeting dry, then throw them into the trash. Hang solvent-soaked rags outdoors to dry—or, better yet, launder them. Never dry or store solvent-soaked materials indoors. They catch fire easily.

WALLCOVERING BASICS

Wallcoverings are an easy way to dress walls with style. Hanging them should come as naturally as painting, but many people are afraid to hang wallcoverings because they think the process is too complicated or the materials too difficult to handle. If you have such fears, this chapter should give you the confidence to plan and execute a wallcovering project with professional-looking results. It presents step-by-step instructions for hanging any type of wallcovering. It explains the principles behind the techniques, so you understand the process thoroughly. Also, it shows you how to select the right materials and use your tools like a pro. Once you understand these fundamentals, you are well along the road to decorating success.

Aside from the design benefits of choosing a tight, monochromatic pattern for this cheery breakfast room, there is a practical advantage too: Pattern mismatches along several edges are inevitable when the wallcovering extends over the ceiling and soffits in addition to the walls, but the mismatches are almost impossible to detect because of the shrewd choice of covering.

# MATERIALS AND TOOLS

"Wallpaper" isn't always paper. Vinyl, fabric, and many other materials (or combinations of materials), in addition to paper, are used to manufacture today's wallcoverings. The following 7 pages will help you to choose the best wallcovering for your project, to purchase the right amount, and to select the proper tools and equipment to apply it.

Selecting Wallcoverings

In thinking about wallcoverings, it's so easy to focus on pattern and color that people may forget to consider the type of wallcovering appropriate for a room. One type doesn't fit all situations. All wallcoverings consist of a combination of materials that gives them their individual degree of durability, washability or scrubbability, stain resistance, abrasion resistance, and colorfastness. The type and amount of use a room receives determines which of these qualities is needed. To understand the differences, it helps to know how wallcoverings are made.

The Basic Composition of Wallcoverings

All wallcoverings have three layers of material.
- The decorative, or surface, layer. This thin top layer consists of the printed design or texture and, possibly, a protective polymer coating. It gives the wallcovering its look.
- The ground, or intermediate, layer. This middle layer gives the wallcovering body and provides the background color for the decorative layer. It ranges from a few mils to 10 mils thick (1 mil = 1/1000 inch). The thicker the wallcovering, the more durable it is.
- The backing, or substrate. This goes against the wall. The ground and backing are the same layer in true papers. Coated, or laminated, wallcoverings have a separate backing made of paper or fabric.

From these layers a wallcovering derives particular characteristics. The list that follows presents some of the terms used to describe them.
- Abrasion resistant: The wallcovering can withstand repeated rubbing, scraping, or scrubbing. (Abrasion resistance and scrubbability are related.) Choose abrasion-resistant wallcoverings for hallways, foyers, kitchens, and other hard-use areas.
- Breathable: The wallcovering lets moisture escape freely, which makes it ideal for high-moisture areas such as bathrooms, kitchens, and laundries. If a wallcovering is not classified as breathable, treat it as if it were a vapor barrier.
- Colorfast: The wallcovering resists fading from exposure to light. Look for colorfastness in a wallcovering to be used in a sunny or bright room.
- Nonbreathable: The wallcovering forms a moisture-resistant barrier.
- Nonstrippable: The wallcovering cannot be removed easily. The paste penetrates the backing, creating a tight bond that can be broken only by wetting or steaming.
- Peelable: The wallcovering's top two layers dry-peel away from its backing, which is intended to become the liner for a new wallcovering. Unfortunately, the backing often loosens as it absorbs moisture from the adhesive of the new wallcovering, and you end up with a lumpy mess. Always remove the backing of a peelable covering before you hang a new wallcovering or paint the wall. Most peelable coverings are paper-backed vinyl.
- Prepasted: The wallcovering has an adhesive-treated backing that is activated by water. You do not have to apply paste. This is the best wallcovering for do-it-yourselfers.
- Scrubbable: The wallcovering withstands scrubbing with a brush and detergent. Use these wallcoverings in high-impact areas such as kitchens, bathrooms, utility rooms, family rooms, and children's bedrooms.
- Stain resistant: The wallcovering does not absorb grease and other stains. Stain resistance and scrubbability go together. Stain-resistant wallcoverings are ideal for hallways, foyers, kitchens, and other areas where fingerprints and food stains abound.
- Strippable: Everyone's favorite, a strippable covering pulls away from the wall without wetting. It leaves a minimum amount of adhesive residue and doesn't damage the surface of the wall.
- Unpasted: The wallcovering has no paste. Paste must be applied uniformly and thoroughly as the wallcovering is hung.
- Washable: The wallcovering withstands occasional sponging with cold water and a detergent, but it will not take repeated hard scrubbing. Washable wallcoverings are good choices for living rooms, dining rooms, bedrooms, and other moderate- to medium-use rooms.

The back of each sample book usually contains complete information about the contents and specific characteristics of the wallcoverings. Check this information against the needs of the room being decorated.

Wallcovering Choices

Wallcoverings are grouped into six main categories and a number of specialty categories, based on the materials used to manufacture each of the three layers. The most popular wallcoverings have some vinyl content. Vinyl's durability, strength, easy handling, and easy upkeep make these wall-coverings especially popular with do-it-yourselfers.

True Paper

Both the backing and the ground layer are paper. The decorative layer is printed directly on the paper. True papers are usually not coated. However, in response to consumer demand, some now have a thin polymer coating that seals in the decorative layer and ground color. Characteristics: unpasted, breathable, washable only if coated.

Coated Paper

The ground layer is a thin coat of vinyl, acrylic, or other plastic. The decorative layer is printed on this coating. Characteristics: prepasted and unpasted types available; comes in strippable, peelable, and nonstrippable types; usually breathable; may be washable.

Coated Fabric

The backing is a fabric, usually a woven scrim. The ground layer is a coat of vinyl or acrylic. The decorative layer is printed on the coating. Characteristics: usually prepasted, strippable, breathable, usually washable, sometimes scrubbable.

Paper-Backed Vinyl

A thick ground layer of solid vinyl film is laminated to a paper backing. The decorative layer is printed directly on this vinyl ground. Together, the decorative layer and ground equal as much as 50 percent of the covering's thickness. Characteristics: prepasted and unpasted, peelable, nonbreathable, washable.

Fabric-Backed Vinyl

The ground layer is a solid vinyl film laminated to a fabric backing, which is about 10 mils thick. The decorative layer is printed on the vinyl. Characteristics: usually unpasted, strippable, nonbreathable, washable and scrubbable, stain and abrasion resistant.

Solid Vinyl

A preformed vinyl film constitutes the ground layer, which is laminated to a fabric or paper backing. The decorative layer is printed on the vinyl. It is more durable and impervious than coverings made with vinyl in other forms. Characteristics: unpasted, nonbreathable, scrubbable, stain and abrasion resistant.

The dense, compact pattern of this wallcovering keeps its large scale from overwhelming the small space.

Wallcovering on the ceiling and skylight well unifies the space.

A sunny breakfast room is animated by a sprightly wallcovering and matching drapery fabric.

Vertical stripes prevent this sweet, rose-sprigged bedroom from being cloying.

The Language of Wallcovering

For definitions of the various types of wallcoverings, see opposite page.

American roll A single roll of wallcovering sized to the 12-inch rule. Standard American rolls yield about 36 square feet of surface material. Contains 25 percent more material than a Euro roll, so you have fewer seams, but its width makes it slightly more difficult to handle.

Blank stock See *Liner paper.*

Bolt Two or three single rolls of wallcovering sold as a continuous length in a single package.

Booking The technique of temporarily folding pasted sides of a wallcovering together so the ends overlap and the sides align.

Border A decorative strip of wallcovering used to accent ceiling lines, chair rails, dadoes, doors, windows, and other architectural features.

Breathable Describes a wallcovering that allows moisture to escape.

Butt-edge seam A wallcovering seam in which the edges of two adjoining drops abut.

Chair rail A strip of decorative wood molding set 32 to 33 inches above the floor.

Color run A batch of wallcovering printed at the same time. Also called dye lot and run number. In covering a room, you should be sure all rolls come from the same color run because colors vary from run to run.

Companion wallcoverings Wallcoverings designed to coordinate and harmonize with one another. Many have companion fabrics too.

Dado A horizontal ornamental border that divides a wall into two sections.

Dead corner An inconspicuous spot where you can place the mismatched last sheets of a wallcovering.

Double-cut seam A wallcovering seam in which the edges of two adjoining sheets are overlapped and then cut through the overlap; then excess materials are removed from both layers and the seam is pressed into place.

Drop A length of wallcovering cut to fit a specific space. A full drop runs from the ceiling to the baseboard and includes allowances for trimming. Also called a sheet.

Drop match A design in which the pattern is staggered rather than straight across. The pattern at the top is the same on every other strip of wallcovering.

Dye lot See *Color run.*

Euro roll A single roll of wallcovering sized in the metric system. Standard Euro rolls yield about 29 square feet of surface material. Its narrower width makes it easier than an American roll to handle, but you get more seams. Today, most wallcoverings are manufactured in Euro rolls.

Frieze A horizontal ornamental border along the top of a room or panel.

Lap seam A seam created by overlapping two strips of a wallcovering.

Level Perfectly horizontal.

Liner paper A special paper, also called blank stock, used to smooth a rough surface to receive a wallcovering.

Pattern match The alignment of wallcovering strips at the edges so that the design makes a continuous horizontal, vertical, or diagonal flow of pattern around the room.

Pattern repeat The distance between identical parts of a wallcovering's pattern in a straight vertical line.

Peelable Describes a wallcovering in which the decorative surface and ground can be separated from the backing. The backing remains on the wall, but should be removed before hanging a new wallcovering or painting the wall.

Plumb A true vertical line on a wall.

Plumb line A weighted chalk line used to establish and mark true vertical on a wall or other surface.

Prepasted Describes a wallcovering that has an adhesive coating applied to its backing by the factory. Activated by dipping in water. These wallcoverings come pretrimmed.

Pretrimmed Describes a wallcovering whose selvages were removed at the factory.

Random match Describes a design in which the pattern doesn't align at vertical edges in a regular fashion.

Repeat The consecutive occurrence of identical elements in a pattern.

Run number See *Color run.*

Scrubbable Describes a wallcovering that can be cleaned with detergent, water, and a brush.

Selvage The blank edge of a wallcovering. Used for markings that maintain registration during printing.

Sheet See *Drop.*

Sliding cut A method of cutting a wallcovering by sliding a sharp knife along the edge of a surface under it.

Square Describes two walls whose sides join one another at true right angles.

Stain-resistant Describes a wallcovering that does not absorb stains.

Straight-across match Describes a design in which the pattern aligns horizontally at single-roll intervals. This means that at the ceiling line, every strip has the same part of the pattern.

Strippable Describes a wallcovering that can be pulled off the wall without first treating it with a wetting agent.

Untrimmed Describes a wallcovering with intact selvages—not factory-trimmed.

Wainscot The lower part of a wall when it has a different covering or finish than the upper part.

Washable Describes a wallcovering that can be cleaned with mild detergent and water applied with a sponge or soft cloth.

Specialty Wallcoverings

Manufacturers produce wallcoverings with many other grounds and backings. These specialty wallcoverings seldom come prepasted. The following are the best known.

• Naturals, which include grass cloth, cork, burlap, and anything else made with organic fibers. They have paper backings. Characteristics: unpasted, breathable.

• Foils, which are made like coated paper or coated fabric, with a thin metallic material in the ground layer. They must be hung on very smooth surfaces and require great care in handling. Characteristics: unpasted, nonbreathable.

• Metalized polyesters, which consist of a vacuum-metalized polyester film laminated to a fabric backing. They have the highly reflective surface of foil without the accompanying stiffness and creasing. They are strong and durable. Mylar™ is a common brand name. Characteristics: unpasted, nonbreathable, scrubbable.

• Flocks, which resemble cut velvet. They consist of shredded fibers laminated onto any of a number of ground materials. Flocks require special handling. Breathability depends on the ground and backing materials.

• Anaglypta®, which is the brand name of a Victorian-style relief wallcovering made of paper or cotton. Its deeply embossed designs look like ornate plasterwork. Available only in white, it must be painted after hanging. Characteristics: unpasted, breathable unless it has been covered with oil-based paint.

• Expanded vinyls, which are made by expanding plastic films under high pressure to produce relief designs. Lincrusta® is a common brand name. Characteristics: unpasted, nonbreathable, scrubbable.

• Hand prints, which are expensive wallcoverings hand-printed with a silk screen. Characteristics: unpasted, washable, breathable.

• Textiles, which includes all fabrics, from corduroy to percale to tapestry. Most are breathable, but some receive a vinyl coating for soil protection. Characteristics: unpasted, breathable if uncoated.

• Commercial wallcoverings, which are designed for use in commercial businesses, institutions, and other public places that receive high traffic. Consult your wallcovering dealer for details.

Buying Wallcoverings

A reputable wallcovering dealer, especially one who serves the interior design trade or who provides interior design services, offers you the best selection from which to choose. This retailer's stock includes a wide range of prices as well as styles. To organize your search so it leads you directly to what you

Seagrass is a natural wallcovering with a delicate texture.

Powder rooms lend themselves to rich and sophisticated wallcovering designs.

The refined, understated pattern of this wallcovering adds richness and sophistication to the bright color.

This vibrant wallcovering pattern forms a lively background for sumptuous entertaining.

want, work closely with the dealer's sales consultant. Be as specific as possible about the room; its size, shape, and use; and the general style or atmosphere you wish to create in it. Take along samples of all fabrics and carpeting in the room. If possible, borrow several sample books at a time and study them in the room at all times of the day. Be prepared to pay a refundable deposit on each book.

How Many Rolls to Buy?

Wallcoverings are priced and measured by the single roll, although they come packaged in double- or triple-roll bolts. Keep this distinction in mind as you figure how much wallcovering you need.

Today most wallcoverings come in Euro rolls, which provide 25 percent less material than American rolls. Find out whether you are buying Euro (metric) rolls or American (nonmetric) rolls. This is the only difference between rolls you need to be concerned about. Then use one of the following formulas to accurately estimate how many rolls to buy.

Remember, however, no simple estimating method is 100 percent accurate. So, don't scrimp in your estimate, and order at least one more bolt than you think you need. Additional bolts ordered after the job starts and single rolls pulled from remnant bins will have dye lots different from that of the original purchase; the colors are unlikely to match.

Usable Yield Method

This method is more accurate because it calculates need based on the repeat length of the pattern. Aligning each strip of wallcovering so the pattern matches the previous strip wastes a certain amount of the roll, depending on the length of the repeat.

1. Using a steel (not cloth) tape measure, measure the height and width of each wall.

Multiply these measurements to get the wall's square footage.

2. For each wall, deduct 15 square feet from the total for each average opening (doors, windows, and such). Measure large or unusual-shaped openings and deduct their exact square footage from the total.

3. Add the adjusted square footages of the walls to get the room's total square footage.

4. Get the repeat length from the wallcovering package or sample book. Check it against the Usable Yield chart below for Euro or American rolls, as appropriate. The repeat length is the number of square feet each roll covers, allowing for pattern matching.

5. Divide the room's total square footage by the usable yield square footage. This is the number of single rolls needed. Round off to the next highest even number of rolls and add an additional bolt.

Usable Yield of Wallcovering Rolls

Usable Yield per Roll (in square feet)

Pattern Repeat Length	Euro Rolls	American Rolls
0–6"	25	32
7–12"	22	30
13–18"	20	27
19–23"	18	25

Understanding Pattern Repeats

Wallcovering patterns repeat themselves at fixed intervals. The distance, along a straight vertical line, between a point in the pattern and an identical point in the next repetition of the pattern is called the pattern repeat length. This distance is always printed on the back of the wallcovering roll. Repeat lengths range from 0 to 48 inches, but most run between 6 and 18 inches. The longer the repeat, the more covering you waste as you match the pattern.

When you can align repetitions of a pattern element horizontally from one strip to the next, the covering is said to have a straight-across match. When you can align repetitions of a pattern element only every other strip, the covering is said to have a drop match.

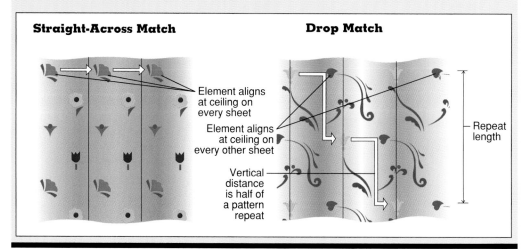

Straight-Across Match

Element aligns at ceiling on every sheet

Element aligns at ceiling on every other sheet

Vertical distance is half of a pattern repeat

Drop Match

Repeat length

Quick Estimating Formula

Follow these steps for an approximate calculation of your needs.

1. Use a steel tape measure (not cloth) to measure the width of each wall, including the doors and windows. Add these figures together and round off to the next highest foot to get the total wall length.

2. Measure the height of the room from floor to ceiling.

3. Using these 2 figures, find the number of rolls you need on the estimating chart at right. Subtract one roll from the total for every 2 standard openings (doors, windows, and the like). Round off to the next highest even number of rolls. Then add an additional bolt.

Coverage for Other Surfaces

Use these methods to calculate the number of rolls needed to cover surfaces such as ceilings, half walls, and borders. Don't scrimp on your estimate. Too much is better than too little.

• Ceilings: Calculate the square footage of a ceiling as if it were a wall, treating the ceiling's shortest dimension as the wall's height. Using the charts, estimate the number of rolls needed based on the square footage. Because you can align the ceiling pattern with the wall pattern on only one wall, allow for additional wallcovering. A dealer can help figure your needs.

• Wainscoting and multiple papers: Make a separate measurement of the area to be

Quick Estimate Charts
Single Rolls of Wallcovering Needed*

Length of Walls	Height of Walls		
	8 Feet	9 Feet	10 Feet
6'	E3, A2	E3, A2	E3, A2
8'	E3, A2–3	E4, A3	E4, A3
10'	E4–5, A3–4	E5, A4	E5, A4
12'	E5, A4	E5, A4	E5, A4
14'	E5, A4	E5, A4	E7, A5
16'	E5–7, A4–5	E7, A5	E8, A6
18'	E7, A5	E8, A6	E8, A6
20'	E8, A6	E8, A6	E9, A7
22'	E8–9, A6–7	E9, A7	E10, A8
24'	E9, A7	E9, A7	E10, A8
26'	E9–10, A7–8	E10, A8	E12, A9
28'	E10, A8	E12, A9	E13, A11
30'	E10, A8	E12, A9	E13, A11
32'	E12, A9	E13, A10	E14, A12
34'	E13, A10	E14, A11	E15, A13
36'	E13, A10	E14, A11	E15, A13
38'	E14, A11	E15, A12	E17, A14
40'	E14, A11	E15, A12	E18, A15
42'	E15, A12	E17, A13	E18, A15
44'	E15, A12	E18, A14	E19, A16
46'	E17, A13	E18, A14	E20, A17
48'	E17, A13	E19, A15	E20, A17
50'	E18, A14	E19, A15	E22, A18

*E=Euro rolls, A=American rolls

Yards of Border

Length of Walls	Border Material Needed
6'	3
8'	3
10'	4
12'	5
14'	5
16'	6
18'	7
20'	7
22'	8
24'	9
26'	9
28'	11
30'	11
32'	12
34'	13
36'	13
38'	14
40'	15
42'	15
44'	16
46'	17
48'	17
50'	18

covered by each wallcovering. Typically, a wainscot, a decorative finish, covers the lower third of a wall's height, which puts its top edge 32 to 33 inches above the floor.

• Borders: Measure the length (not the square footage) of the area to be covered in yards—borders come in 5-yard rolls. If you plan to miter corners, order an extra roll to cover cutting and waste.

Check Your Purchase

Manufacturers aim to produce first-quality goods, but mistakes do occur. Open and examine each bolt, except the extra bolt, as soon as you receive the wallcovering. (Leave the extra bolt unopened so you can return it if you don't need it to complete the job. Dealers accept only unopened bolts for refunds.)

First, check each bolt's dye lot number. They must be the same. If they aren't, exchange them for a new batch. Now, open and reroll each bolt, checking for printing flaws as the covering passes. Look for

consistency of pattern, color, and surface finish. Also look for ink blobs or smudges, streaks, wrinkling, pattern shifts, or obvious misalignments. You selected your wallcovering based on its material composition and wear qualities. Check for them with these simple tests.

Water Drop Test

This tests for a vinyl coating. Place a few drops of water at the top of the bolt on the pattern side. If the water doesn't soak into the covering within 5 minutes, the covering has a vinyl coating.

Match Test

Cut one full pattern repeat off the top of the first bolt. Use this piece as a test strip. Match its pattern with the top of all the bolts. They should align (according to the type of pattern match, straight-across or drop). Also check the direction of the pattern on each bolt—it should flow diagonally toward the lead (top left) edge. This rule helps you determine which way is up on a pattern: Flowers grow up and shadows fall under flowers and other objects. If you find a reversed roll, open and reroll it correctly. Secure the new roll with several #14 rubber bands. Finally, compare the colors on the test strip with those on the other bolts. They should match.

Paste Test

Cut the test strip into 2 pieces. Wet a spot on the back of one piece. If it becomes slippery and tacky, it is prepasted; if not, it is unpasted. If it is prepasted, put 2 drops of iodine on 2 dry spots. If it turns brown, the paste is starch-based; it will need to be soaked 15 to 30 seconds. If the iodine spots turn purple, the paste is cellulose-based; soak it only 1 to 15 seconds.

Wear Test

With your fingernail, scrape along the top edge of the other test strip. If the decorative layer peels or degrades under this pressure, the covering is not abrasion resistant. If the covering does not have the qualities you specified, take all the bolts back to your retailer for full replacement.

Tools, Equipment, and Other Materials

Having the right tools, materials, and equipment is as important as choosing the right wallcovering. They make the job go more smoothly and help you achieve professional results.

• Adhesives: For unpasted wallcoverings, clear, nonstaining premixed vinyl paste; for repairs and special installations, vinyl-to-vinyl or seam-and-border paste.

• Apron: Tool (with plenty of pouches).

• Broad knife, 6-inch: Use as a cutting guide, to work wallcoverings into narrow spaces, and to score or cut them.

• Buckets, 5-gallon size: Line with plastic trash bags to make trash receptacles. Use unlined to hold rinse water or paste.

• Carpenter's square: Use as a guide for measuring and cutting.

• Ladders: Your most important tools (see page 23).

• Paint screen: For working paste into a roller cover.

• Paste syringe: For injecting adhesive into air-pocket bubbles.

• Paste whip or propeller on drill: For mixing paste.

• Pencils, #1: For lightly marking measurements on walls.

• Razor knives, or utility knives, with lots of new blades: For cutting and trimming.

• Roller cover, ½-inch synthetic nap, on head with extension pole: These tools are for rolling paste on unpasted covering.

• Rubber bands, #14 size: To secure back-rolled strips of covering.

• Scissors: For cutting into angles and trimming margins.

• Seam roller, rubber or foam (not wood): For sealing seams.

• Smoothing brush, ½-inch: For smoothing paper against the wall.

• Sponges: For cleaning all surfaces. Ceramic tile sponges are best.

• Stopwatch or watch with sweep second hand: For timing the soaking period of prepasted wallcoverings.

• Straightedge: Use as a substitute for a carpenter's square.

• Tape measure, steel: Buy one with a 1-inch-wide blade, at least 16 feet long.

• Towels: For carrying booked strips and for drying.

• Water tray: For wetting prepasted wallcoverings.

• Worktable: Make one with a 4 X 8 sheet of ½-inch plywood propped on sawhorses, or set the plywood on top of another table.

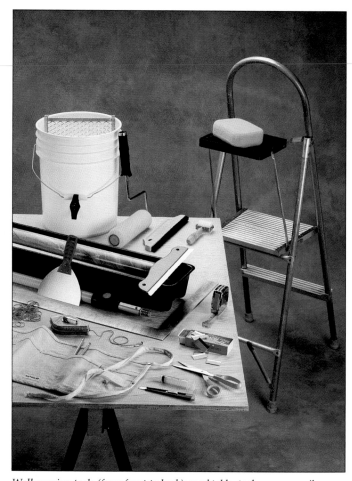

Wallcovering tools (from front to back): worktable, tool apron, pencils, razor knife, glue syringe, scissors, rubber bands, chalk line, single-edge razor blades, carpenter's square, 6-inch broad knife, roller extension handle, tape measure, water tray, smoothing blade, watch, bucket, roller screen, paint roller, smoothing brush, seam roller, step ladder, and tile sponge.

PREPARING THE WALLS

You did much of the preparation work required for hanging a wallcovering when you repaired and cleaned the room (see second chapter, page 22). The final steps of preparing walls (and the ceiling, if you are covering it) are to develop a layout plan, check for rough surfaces, and prime the walls.

Planning a Room Layout

A professional wallcovering job depends upon a well-planned layout that indicates where each sheet will be on the walls. Without such planning, you may end up with awkward seam locations, strips of wallcovering too narrow for proper adhesion, mismatches in conspicuous places, or a strong wallcovering pattern that feels out of balance with the room's focal point. To avoid such problems, let three principles guide your planning.

• Start the layout (not necessarily the installation) at the vertical centerline of the room's focal-point wall (see the next section). From this starting point the pattern will flow evenly across this wall and on around the room.

• Put the last seam, which usually mismatches, in the most inconspicuous spot in the room, called the dead corner. Common dead corners include corners behind doors, the header space above the room's entrance door, and hidden alcoves.

• Reduce the number of full-length seams in the room by planning to place seams near the center of windows and doors. However, try to leave at least half a sheet—or at least a strip wider than 6 inches—on each side of a door or window.

The first layout you develop may not satisfy all of these principles. There are other factors, such as corners, to consider. You may need to make adjustments through a process of trial and error. The starting point, however, should always be the centerline of the focal-point wall.

Locate the Focal Point

To begin the layout, stand in the doorway and look for the room's focal point. The focal point is probably one of the following.

• The first wall you see as you enter the room. The centerline runs down its middle.

• The room's main window or windows (often located opposite the door). If there is only one window, no matter what its size, it becomes the focal point and the centerline runs down its center. If there is more than one window but they are on different walls, the larger window is the focal point. If there are two or more windows set close together or side by side, the focal-point centerline lies midway between them. If you have corner windows, or windows near the corner, on two adjoining walls, they make a focal corner. The centerline runs through the center of the window closest to that corner, or through the largest window.

• The portion of wall above a fireplace.

• The largest section of exposed wall in a bathroom or kitchen.

• The main section of wall in a kitchen eating area.

Your layout starts at the vertical centerline of this wall. Once you identify the focal point of the room, use a #1 pencil to lightly mark the centerline, at eye level. This becomes the starting point for planning a trial layout of sheet positions.

Plan the Sheet Positions

1. Measure the width of the wallcovering and add ⅛ inch to allow for expansion when it is wet. This is the layout dimension, the width of most sheets as you hang them, except when you go around corners. If, for example, the

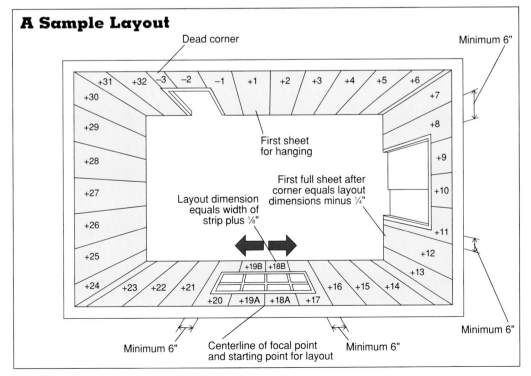

A Sample Layout

Dead corner

Minimum 6"

+31 +32 −3 −2 −1 +1 +2 +3 +4 +5 +6 +7 +8 +9 +10 +11 +12 +13 +14 +15 +16 +17 +18A +19A +20 +21 +22 +23 +24 +25 +26 +27 +28 +29 +30 +18B +19B

First sheet for hanging

First full sheet after corner equals layout dimensions minus ¼"

Layout dimension equals width of strip plus ⅛"

Minimum 6"

Minimum 6"

Centerline of focal point and starting point for layout

Minimum 6"

wallcovering is 21 inches wide, there will be a seam every 21⅛ inches on the walls. At inside corners (see illustrations on page 83), subtract ¼ inch from this measurement for the first sheet on the new wall. (The 21⅛-inch-wide sheet becomes 20⅞ inches wide.) At outside corners, subtract ½ inch from the first sheet's width. (The 21⅛-inch-wide sheet becomes 20⅝ inches wide.)

2. Decide whether you want to center the first sheet over the centerline or to butt it to the centerline. Measure for both possibilities, working first to the right from the centerline to the corner and then to the left, then choose the position that avoids too narrow a strip at the corners or adjacent to the windows and that gives you the fewest seams. After choosing the best layout, use a #1 pencil to mark the seam locations at eye level on the wall.

3. Measure and mark the seams for the rest of the room, working from the corners of the focal-point wall to the dead corner.

Number the Sheet Positions

Number the sheet positions in the order in which you plan to hang the sheets. You don't necessarily want to start at the centerline. For instance, you don't want to start hanging around a window or other architectural feature. Instead, you want the first two or three sheets to be full-length drops. This helps you establish a hanging rhythm before you start working around windows and doors. Number the positions as follows.

1. Look for the first area to the right of the door where at least 3 full sheets can be hung, and mark the wall with a +1 where that sheet will hang.

2. Working from left to right, continue numbering the sheet positions around the room to the dead corner (+2, +3, and so on). When you come to wide windows or other openings where you must split the sheet in two, label the upper section A (+5A, for example) and the bottom section B (+5B, for example).

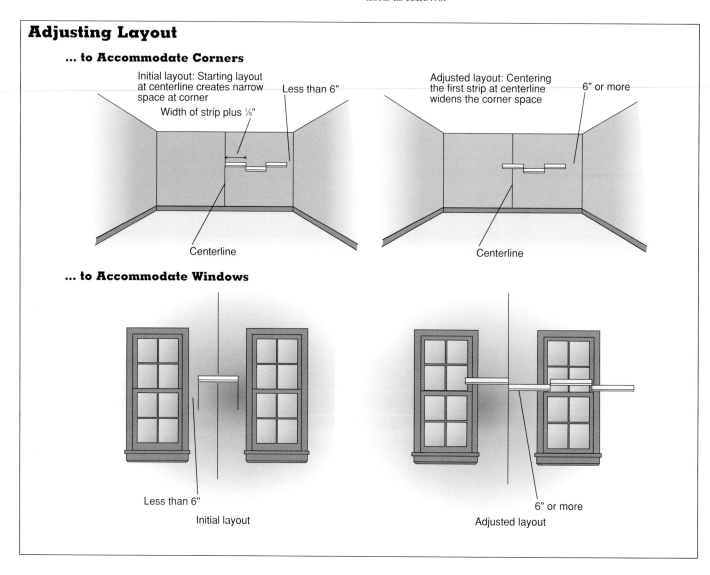

Adjusting Layout

... to Accommodate Corners

Initial layout: Starting layout at centerline creates narrow space at corner

Width of strip plus ⅛"

Less than 6"

Centerline

Adjusted layout: Centering the first strip at centerline widens the corner space

6" or more

Centerline

... to Accommodate Windows

Less than 6"

Initial layout

6" or more

Adjusted layout

Review the safety procedures and the tips for how to use ladders in the second chapter (pages 23 and 27). Hanging wallcoverings involves a lot of movement, so it's important to thoroughly secure ladders and platforms, use them correctly, and be careful at all times.

You can hang a wallcovering by yourself, but the job is much easier if you have a partner. Then one person, the activator, pastes and books the covering while the other, the hanger, hangs it. Before you begin, decide who will do each job. This establishes a rhythm so you work efficiently and don't get in each other's way.

If you are not working with a helper, be sure to plan your work carefully or you may end up wasting time, or pasted wallpaper, or both.

3. Return to the left side of sheet +1 and number the sheet positions, using negative numbers (-1, -2, and so on), until you reach the dead corner.

4. Write each sheet number and the sheet's exact length on a notepad. If you are going to cover only part of a wall, such as a wainscot, see page 71 for instructions on measuring partial drops.

Planning a Ceiling Layout

Consider the ceiling's shortest dimension to be the same as a wall's height. This gives you shorter strips, which are easier to work with.

1. To find the ceiling's centerline, lightly mark on the ceiling the midpoint of each long wall and connect the marks with a faint chalk line.

2. Decide whether to center the first sheet over this line or butt it to this line (see pages 73 and 74). Plan the strips from the center out to the ends in whichever way gives you the fewest seams.

Note: Always hang the ceiling before the walls (see page 86).

Completing Wall Preparation

Before you hang the covering, you must smooth out uneven surfaces—especially of paneled, tiled, or textured walls—and prime the walls. You should also turn off the power to any outlets or switches around which you will be hanging wallcovering.

Smooth Rough Surfaces

There are three ways to smooth rough walls, each with advantages and disadvantages.

• Cover them with liner paper, or blank stock. The best are made of compressed fibers. Liners hang like wallcoverings (follow directions on pages 80 to 88), with one exception: The seams either run horizontally or they run vertically out of plumb, so they don't coincide with the wallcovering's vertical seams. Liners are a quick fix but leave much to be desired for a long-lasting installation. The rough surface underneath often punctures them, and they can absorb moisture from the wallcovering's primer/sealer and adhesive, causing them to pull away from the wall.

• Remove the texture (see page 26). This gives you a better surface, but it is a messy process.

• Float the wall (see page 25). This gives you the smoothest surface, but it is hard work.

Prime the Walls

Forget the word *sizing.* Today walls are prepared with one of the premixed primer/sealers made specifically for use under wallcoverings. They create a surface film that improves the wallcovering's adhesion. These products come in oil- and acrylic-based formulas and are applied with a roller, just like paint. The water-based acrylic formulas clean up with water and are easier to apply. A pigmented oil-based primer/sealer prevents paint colors from showing through lightweight coverings. Your dealer can help you pick the primer/sealer that is best suited to your wallcovering.

How you prepare walls for a wallcovering depends on whether they are painted or unpainted.

Painted Walls

General preparation of the room includes scrubbing painted walls (see page 33). Apply the primer/sealer over the scrubbed walls as if applying a coat of paint. Let dry 2 to 4 hours before hanging the wallcovering.

Unpainted Wallboard

Tape, sand, and otherwise prepare the wallboard to receive paint as described on page 29. Then seal the walls by following the next three steps.

1. Apply a coat of oil-based undercoat. Let dry 8 hours.

2. Sand the wall lightly with 120-grit sandpaper. Vacuum up the dust. Re-mark the layout seams.

3. Apply the primer/sealer formulated for your wallcovering. Let it dry 2 to 4 hours before starting to hang your wallcovering.

Unpainted Plaster Walls

Allow new plaster walls to cure at least thirty days. Then seal the walls by following the next three steps.

1. Apply a coat of oil-based wall sealer and let it dry thoroughly.

2. Sand the wall lightly with 120-grit sandpaper. Vacuum up the dust. Re-mark the layout seams.

3. Apply an oil-based wallcovering sealer formulated for your wallcovering. Let dry 2 to 4 hours before hanging the wallcovering.

Use the sequence this section will outline to hang every wallcovering, no matter what its composition, no matter where it goes. These steps give you a systematic way to organize the job so you complete it with a minimal amount of time, effort, and wasted wallcovering. Master these basic techniques and you can handle any and every wallcovering job.

Cutting the Material

First, familiarize yourself with your pattern's match and repeat. They determine how you cut the wallcovering. No matter what the pattern, the match and repeat must mate from one sheet to the next.

Determine the Pattern

Textured wallcoverings and wallcoverings with scattered or random designs have no visible pattern match or repeat. You can cut the sheets from the roll continuously—the top edge of a sheet begins at the cut for the bottom edge of the previous sheet. With all other designs, which have either straight-across or drop pattern matches (see page 70), you have to carefully align and match the pattern before you cut each sheet. Plan to have a major pattern element fall just below the ceiling line. With a straight-across match, this element will be at the top of every sheet. With a drop match, the element will align at the ceiling on every other sheet.

Find the Starting Point

Taking into account the pattern match and repeat, establish the ceiling line (starting point) on the pattern. (If you're covering the ceiling, you may want the pattern to run continuously from the ceiling down onto one wall. Cover the ceiling [see page 86], then establish the ceiling line of the covering for the walls, so the pattern continues.) To do this, you need a place to roll out some wallcovering, so you might as well set up your worktable for cutting, pasting, and booking now. You need a sheltered place (no rain, wind, or sun) large enough to allow you to comfortably walk around a 4- by 8-foot table, where water spills and other messes won't be a problem. Garages, carports, and unfinished basements are ideal.

1. Temporarily attach the water tray to one end of the table by stapling along the lip of the tray, so it can hold a bolt of material while you roll it out, face up, the length of the table.

2. Stand back 3 to 4 feet and squint at the covering. This blurs the pattern's minor details so you see its major elements and their rhythm. Plan so a full major element falls just below the ceiling line; never

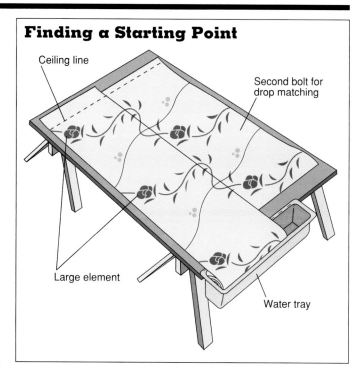

Finding a Starting Point

Ceiling line

Second bolt for drop matching

Large element

Water tray

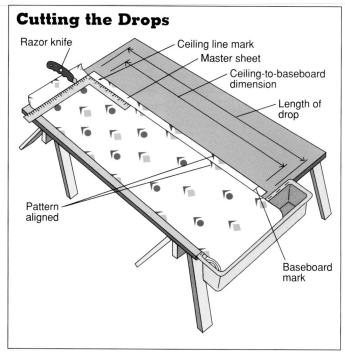

Cutting the Drops

Razor knife

Ceiling line mark

Master sheet

Ceiling-to-baseboard dimension

Length of drop

Pattern aligned

Baseboard mark

cut through a major element at the ceiling line. If possible, keep a little plain background area above the element to mask unevenness where the ceiling and wall meet.

3. If your pattern has a drop match, roll out a second bolt on the table and place it beside the first, with the patterns matching. Use the same squinting technique to find the best breaking point across both sheets.

4. If you plan to hang a border at the top of the wall, plan to have the major element fall just below it.

Cut the Drops

It is important to cut all the drops in sequence, so the pattern matches all around the room. To prevent confusion, cut them all in one session. You need a steel tape measure, a carpenter's square, and several razor knives with plenty of replacement razor blades. Don't measure with a yardstick or a ruler.

Start with sheet +1 and cut it and succeeding full drops according to the instructions that follow. When you come to a split sheet (such as above and below a window), follow the directions in the next section; for partial drops, such as wainscoting, see page 82.

1. Check the sheet lengths recorded on your notepad. Select the longest to be the ceiling-to-baseboard dimension for sheet +1.

2. Lightly mark the ceiling line on the edge at the top of the sheet pulled out on the table. Place the inside of the elbow of the carpenter's square on this mark. Its 2-inch-wide arm adds a 2-inch top margin, to allow for uneven ceilings, without extra measuring. Holding the square firmly in place, cut the wallcovering along the outside edge with your knife, or tear it with your hands.

3. From your first mark, measure down the ceiling-to-baseboard dimension and mark this point on the edge. Place the inside corner of the square's elbow at this point, which will create a 2-inch bottom margin to allow for uneven floors. Holding the square firmly in place, cut or tear the wallcovering along the outside edge. You have created a master sheet.

4. The master sheet becomes a cutting guide. Slide it ½ inch away from you so one edge will be exposed as you cut sheets on top of it. Unroll some covering over the master sheet and align the pattern. Check for the correct ceiling line point. Then match it to the master sheet, lay the square in place, and cut sheet +2 as you did the master sheet.

5. Cut all the sheets consecutively, stacking them on top of the master sheet. Weight the sheets if they tend to curl.

6. When all the sheets are cut, turn the stack over and lightly pencil the location number in the upper left-hand corner on the back of each sheet. For a drop match, mark them +1-O for odd, +2-E for even, +3-O, +4-E, and so on, to indicate the alternating alignments.

7. Back-roll each sheet, from bottom to top, with the backside out. Secure with #14 rubber bands.

Cut Split Sheets

Sheets hung above and below openings present a special problem. You waste material if you just cut a full sheet and discard the portion that would cover the opening. Instead, cut the top and bottom sections separately.

Cut the top section first. Align and cut the top edge as you would a full sheet, allowing for a 2-inch margin above the ceiling line. Measure for the bottom cut, add 2 inches and tear across the sheet at that point (using a knife risks damaging the sheets underneath). Mark the piece with its position number and an *A*.

Before unrolling more covering for the bottom piece, use the master sheet to find where the bottom of the opening will align on the pattern. (If the pattern has a drop match and the split sheet is an even number, use sheet +2-E as the master sheet.) Measure up from the bottom of the master sheet 2 inches for the margin, then a distance equal to the lower wall section. Mark the master sheet edge at this point. Then unroll some covering so that the pattern near the top edge matches the pattern of the master sheet at the point

Can you locate the dead corner of this layout? The small, intricate pattern makes it inconspicuous.

where you marked it. Allowing for at least 2 inches of margin, measure down from this point a distance equal to the lower wall section, add 2 inches, and tear across it. Mark this piece with its position number and a *B*.

Setting Up the Job

Now unstaple the water tray, cover the table with a plastic sheet, and put the water tray at one end. Then gather all the hanging tools, including the ladder, in the room where you'll hang the wallcovering. Cover the floor along the walls with a 4- by 16-foot drop cloth runner and bring two 5-gallon buckets into the room. Line one with plastic bags to serve as a trash bucket. Fill the other with rinse water.

Pasting and Booking

Booking (folding) keeps the paste from drying out and keeps it away from everything until the covering gets to the wall. You will paste and book the sheets in the order in which they are numbered. Keeping them in order prevents confusion when hanging. The instructions that follow call for a rest period— this will give the paste time to soak into the material, improving its adhesion, and also give the covering time to relax (expand) so it is pliable. The procedures for pasted wallcoverings are little different from those for unpasted.

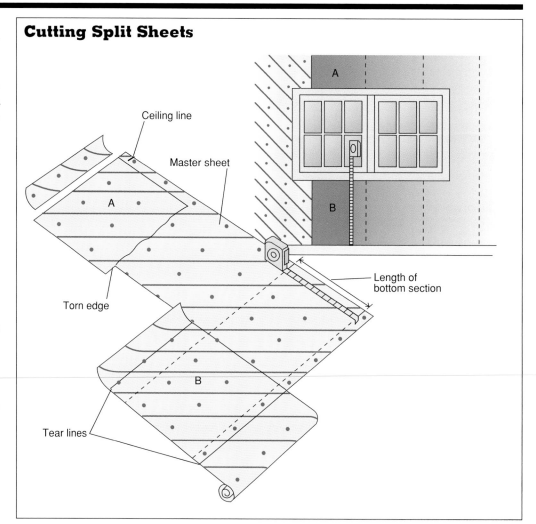

Cutting Split Sheets

Ceiling line

Master sheet

A

Torn edge

Tear lines

B

A

B

Length of bottom section

Prepasted Wallcoverings

1. Fill the water tray three-fourths full of lukewarm water—warmer water will cook the adhesive and over-expand the paper, colder water won't penetrate and activate the adhesive.

2. Remove the rubber band and loosen sheet +1 so water can get between the layers. Place the sheet in the tray and let it soak the recommended time, timing it precisely with a stopwatch. Oversoaking dissolves the adhesive; under-soaking doesn't give the water time to penetrate it.

3. Slowly pull three-fourths of the strip out of the tray, paste side up. Quickly check the back for uniform wetness, and splash dry spots with water from the tray.

4. Fold the top edge of the strip down to the middle, paste sides together. Align the edges and smooth, but do not crease the fold.

5. Slowly pull out the rest of the sheet. Check it for wetness and wet dry spots as necessary. Fold the bottom up and tuck it under the top edge so the ends overlap about 1 inch. Align and smooth as you did the top section.

6. Fold the top fold over until it touches the bottom fold. Repeat. The sheet is now booked. Set it aside for 3 to 5 minutes while you wet and book more strips. (If properly booked, a strip can sit for as long as 10 to 15 minutes without drying out.)

7. Clean the plastic sheet with clear water and a sponge, and towel-dry. Soak and book 3 additional sheets, stacking them on top of one another and cleaning the tabletop each time.

8. Flip the stack over. This puts the first sheet back on top. Wrap the stack in a towel and carry it to the room.

Wetting and Booking Prepasted Wallcovering

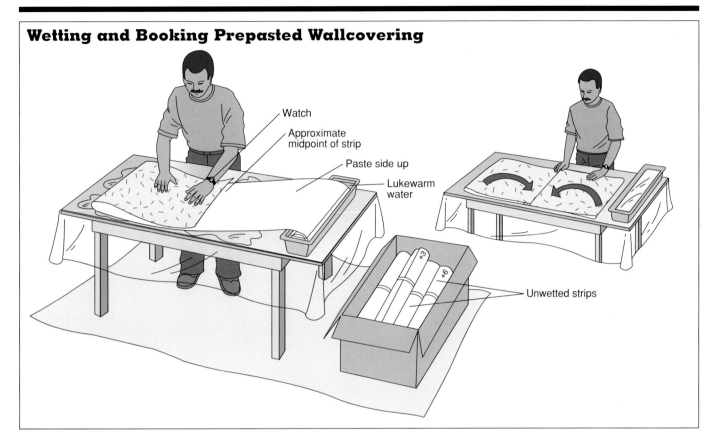

Watch

Approximate midpoint of strip

Paste side up

Lukewarm water

Unwetted strips

Unpasted Wallcoverings

Use a clear, nonstaining pre-mixed vinyl wallcovering paste. Read the manufacturer's instructions. They usually recommend thinning the paste to a spreading consistency, as follows. In a 5-gallon bucket, mix 2 to 3 cups water into 2½ gallons premixed paste until it has the consistency of pancake batter. Use a paste whip or a propeller mounted on a power drill to mix the ingredients. Let paste stand overnight so excess air escapes.

Apply the paste the next day, with a roller fitted with a ½-inch-thick synthetic nap cover. Load the roller with paste as you would with paint (see page 44).

1. Unroll sheet +1 face down on the table. Roll paste along the edges on the top three-fourths of the sheet.

2. Then roll paste across the width of the covering, working from the center out to the edge of the area to be pasted. Apply it in overlapping *M* strokes until you thoroughly coat the top three-quarters of the sheet. Finish by rolling one more coat along the edges.

3. Book the top the same as for prepasted covering. Paste the remainder of the sheet, book, and set it aside. Clean the plastic with clear water and a sponge, and towel-dry.

4. Paste and book just one more sheet. Unpasted coverings absorb the paste's moisture, causing it to dry out quickly.

5. Flip the sheets over so the first is on top. Slip them into a plastic bag and carry them to the room.

Pasting Unpasted Wallcovering

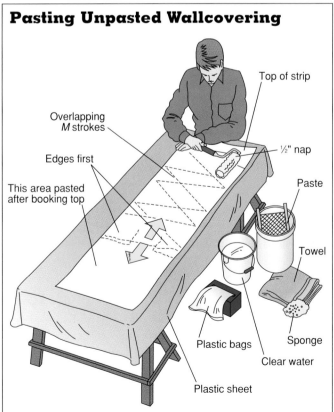

Overlapping *M* strokes

Edges first

This area pasted after booking top

Top of strip

½" nap

Paste

Towel

Sponge

Clear water

Plastic bags

Plastic sheet

HANGING THE WALLCOVERING

You've planned the layout. You've prepped the walls. You've cut, pasted, and booked the sheets. The stage is set. It is time to hang the wallcovering.

The Three Rules

Three general rules govern the hanging of wallcoverings.

•You need a plumb line on each wall to maintain true vertical on each wall.

•You *cut* inside corners and *wrap* outside corners.

•You never overlap—almost never. Follow these rules to achieve a professional-looking wallcovering job.

Hanging Straight Drops

This process works best with two people. While the activator pastes and books the first few sheets, the hanger readies the room for hanging. This includes snapping a plumb line to mark the right-hand seam (if you are right-handed) of the master sheet. Use white or yellow chalk so the line won't show through the seam. Locate the seam mark you made earlier on the wall. Use your carpenter's square to extend it to the ceiling line. Tack the weighted plumb line at this point. Don't touch the weighted string until it stops swinging. Then hold the string taut at the bottom and snap the line. This light chalk mark gives you the true vertical line for that wall. Each sheet on the wall will be hung according to this accurate line. *Note:* Every time you turn a corner, you must snap a new plumb line

to establish a true vertical line on the new wall.

Hanging the First Straight Drop

A sheet of wallcovering becomes a drop when you hang it on a wall. You learn an important secret with this first drop—namely, a wallcovering goes on more easily and adheres more firmly to the wall when you handle it gently. You don't need to push, pull, shove, or pressure it into place to get a good seal. Rough han-

dling only stretches the material and pushes the paste out of place. This, in turn, causes the sheets to pull away from one another as they dry, so the seam becomes visible. Also, it causes the corners to pull away from walls after they have dried.

You learn something else too: the basic hanging technique. Every sheet of wallcovering, no matter what the material or where it is being hung, goes on the wall in the same way, always in the same order. Before you begin, place the ladder directly in front of the space where the first sheet will go. Put the broad knife, smoothing brush, seam roller, and extra razor blades in your apron pockets. Put several razor knives in your back or

hip pocket so they don't get misplaced. Remember to change blades often so you always work with a sharp knife. This gives you the clean cuts you need for a professional-looking job. You are ready to hang sheet +1.

1. Climb up on the ladder and unfold the top portion. The folded bottom acts as a weight to hold the sheet straight. Align the sheet at the ceiling line so its edge falls directly over the plumb line. The top 2-inch margin overlaps the ceiling.

2. Using your hands, place the edge directly over the plumb line down to the middle of the wall.

3. Use the smoothing brush to push the sheet into the ceiling line so the 2-inch margin

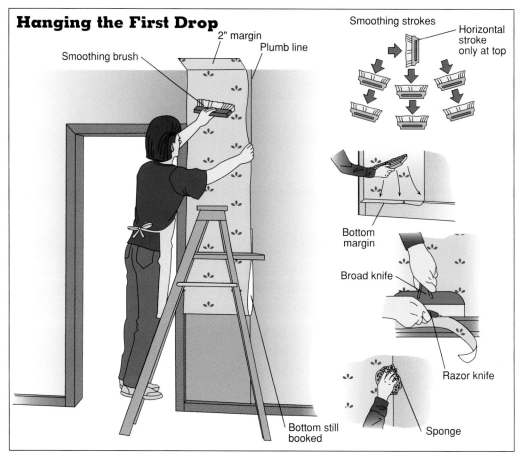

Hanging the First Drop

Smoothing brush · 2" margin · Plumb line · Smoothing strokes · Horizontal stroke only at top · Bottom margin · Broad knife · Razor knife · Sponge · Bottom still booked flaps over onto the ceiling. Then press the top section into place with horizontal, then downward strokes of your brush (see illustration on opposite page).

4. Climb down and move the ladder out of the way. Open the bottom half of the sheet and repeat this process, using the smoothing brush to push the strip against the wall and down into the baseboard seam. The bottom 2-inch margin overlaps the baseboard.

5. Using the broad knife as a guide, trim off the excess margins at the ceiling line and baseboard with the razor knife.

6. Gently lift the edge and wipe away the chalk line. Smooth the edge back into place with your brush. Then

brush over the entire sheet one more time. If some bubbles and wrinkles won't work out, don't worry about them at this point. Most will disappear as the covering shrinks during drying.

7. Gently run the seam roller over the edges. Do not bear down hard—force pushes paste from behind the seams and creates furrows in the covering.

8. Wipe down the entire surface with clear water and a sponge. Towel-dry.

Hanging Additional Straight Drops

Just as you hung the first drop, hang the second against it; make sure the pattern matches and use one of the seams described next. Continue hang-

ing sheets—checking the vertical, horizontal and diagonal pattern lines across the seams to make sure the sheets are properly aligned—until you reach the dead corner.

Seams

The three basic wallcovering seams are the butt seam, the double-cut seam, and the lap seam.

•Butt seam: The most common wallcovering seam. The sheets butt snugly against one another, edge to edge, with no overlap. Be careful not to stretch the material; otherwise, the seams will pull away from one another as the covering dries.

•Double-cut seam: The next most common wallcovering seam. Each sheet slightly overlaps the preceding sheet. Using a carpenter's square or a straightedge as a guide, cut through both layers with the knife. Make the cut from the ceiling to the baseboard without cutting into the wall. Throw away the scrap on the top sheet. Carefully lift the edge of the top sheet and pull out the scrap from the bottom sheet. Gently smooth the top sheet back into place with your brush; roll the seam.

•Lap seam: This is an old-fashioned seam, and the one of last resort. One sheet simply overlaps another and is left that way. If the wallcovering contains vinyl, carefully lift

Making a Butt Seam

No overlapping

Seam

Seam roller

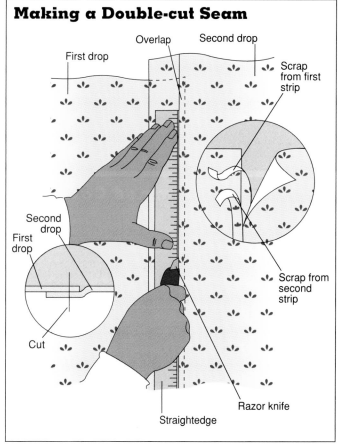

Making a Double-cut Seam

First drop

Overlap

Second drop

Scrap from first strip

Second drop

First drop

Cut

Scrap from second strip

Straightedge

Razor knife

the top seam and apply vinyl-to-vinyl paste to its backside. Gently smooth the top sheet back into place with your smoothing brush and roll the seam.

Hanging Part of a Wall

Partial drops are hung in the same way as full-length drops. However, unless the room has a chair-rail molding, you need a horizontal guideline for the top or bottom edge, as appropriate. Orient this guideline to the ceiling.

Typically, walls are divided 32 to 33 inches from the floor, or approximately one third the wall's height. Subtract this from the wall's full height to get the height of the upper section of the wall. (If you plan to use a border with an upper wallcovering, subtract the border's width from the section's height.) Measure this distance down from the ceiling at both ends of the wall and lightly mark these points. Stretch a chalk line between the marks and snap a guideline marking the border between the base and upper sections of the wall. The guideline will serve as the ceiling line for a wainscot (lower wall) and as the baseboard for an upper wallcovering. Let each drop's top or bottom margin overlap the guideline. Snap a new guideline on top of the covering. Use your carpenter's square as a guide to trim the covering along this guideline, or cover the seam with a border and trim as described on page 90.

Hanging Two Coverings on a Wall

Make your guideline the same as for a half-wall installation. Hang the upper drops first, letting them overlap this guideline. Snap a new guideline in the same location but on top of the upper covering. Hang the base covering so it overlaps the guideline and the upper covering. Snap another guideline in the same location. Using your carpenter's square as a cutting guide, make a double-cut seam (see page 81) along this line. Let the coverings dry thoroughly. If desired, cover the seam with a border (see page 91).

Hanging Around Corners and Openings

All corners, windows, doors, and other openings and obstructions require special handling.

Covering Inside Corners

Walls are not plumb and square. That's why you can't push a wallcovering into an inside corner and lap it onto the next wall without losing the true vertical. You must cut it to fit into the corner, as well as hide misalignments in an inconspicuous place. First, unfold the booked sheet and rebook so you are sure all edges are precisely parallel. Then follow the next four steps.

Making a Lap Seam

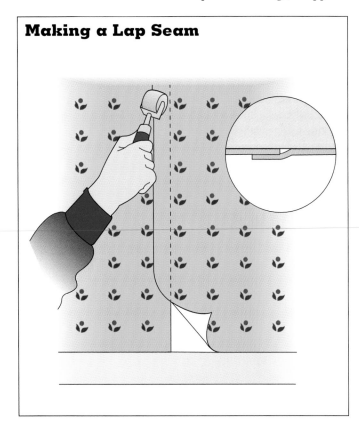

Trimming Untrimmed Coverings

Although uncommon, untrimmed wallcoverings do exist, most often in specialty wallcoverings. You must trim off their blank selvages. Work quickly because untrimmed coverings have little or no vinyl content and dry out quickly. Use a separate cutting board.

1. Paste and book each sheet as usual and let stand until the paste is tacky. Test the sheet with your finger—it is ready when it moves slightly but does not slip. You cannot hang a slippery sheet: It slides when you double-cut the seam.

2. Hang sheet +1 on the wall so the selvage overlaps the plumb line. Using your carpenter's square as a cutting guide, trim off the selvage as soon as the sheet is stable on the wall.

3. Hang sheet +2 so its selvage overlaps sheet +1 by ⅜ inch. Precisely match the pattern. Using your carpenter's square as a guide, make a double-cut seam (see page 81) on the pattern, just inside the top selvage line. Finish as usual. Repeat these steps with each additional sheet. Reroll the seams after you've hung 3 or 4 sheets.

Hanging an Inside Corner

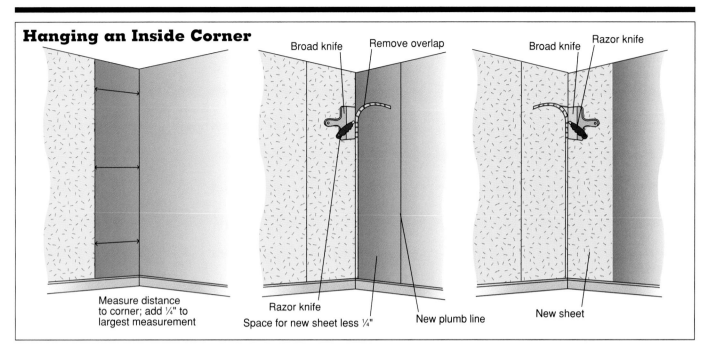

Broad knife — Remove overlap

Broad knife — Razor knife

Measure distance to corner; add ¼" to largest measurement

Razor knife

Space for new sheet less ¼"

New plumb line

New sheet

Hanging an Outside Corner

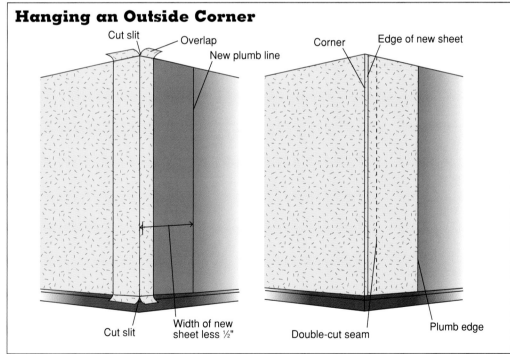

Cut slit — Overlap — New plumb line

Corner — Edge of new sheet

Cut slit

Width of new sheet less ½"

Double-cut seam

Plumb edge

1. When you have less than the width of one sheet before a corner, measure the remaining wall at the ceiling line, midpoint, and baseboard. Add ¼ inch to the largest measurement. Mark this width on the booked sheet (be sure you know which is the top edge) and, using your carpenter's square as a guide, cut through all the layers at once. Don't discard the leftover piece.

2. Butt the cut sheet to the preceding sheet and smooth it as firmly as possible into the corner. Score down the corner line with your broad knife or razor knife. Strip away and discard the waste flap.

3. Measure the width of the leftover piece. Subtract ¼ inch from this measurement and snap a plumb line on the new wall this distance from the corner.

4. Place the leftover piece directly over the new plumb line. Use your smoothing brush to work it into the corner, overlapping ¼ inch onto the first wall. Again, score down the corner line with your broad knife or razor knife. Strip away and discard the waste flap.

Covering Outside Corners

Again, because walls aren't square and plumb, you must snap a new plumb line and adjust the wallcovering to vertical after you wrap the corner.

1. Hang the drop that goes around the corner as usual, smoothing it up to and around the corner edge. Make slits in the top and bottom margins where they bend around the corner. This eases the covering so it can wrap smoothly around the corner.

2. Subtract ½ inch from the next sheet's measurement and snap a plumb line on the new wall this distance from the corner.

3. Set the sheet directly on this plumb line. Smooth into place, letting the covering lap over the existing covering at the corner edge.

4. Using a carpenter's square or a straightedge as a guide, make a double-cut seam (see page 81) to remove the overlap.

Ending at an Outside Corner

Use this technique when you don't want to cover the wall adjoining an outside corner. Hang the covering as usual, only let the excess hang out past the corner instead of smoothing it down. Hold the excess covering taut with one hand and, holding your knife at a 45-degree angle and cutting from the face side, make a sliding cut down the edge of the wall. This sliding cut makes a clean, precise corner edge that won't fray or peel away.

Hanging Around Trimmed Doors and Windows

Do not try to cut a sheet in advance to fit around doors or windows—or fireplaces, bookcases, or cabinets either. Instead, let a full-length drop hang over the opening.

1. Hang the drop as usual, keeping the bottom half booked. With your smoothing brush press the covering against the top and sides of the opening's trim molding. At this point, the covering hangs over the opening.

2. If there is a large amount of covering over the opening,

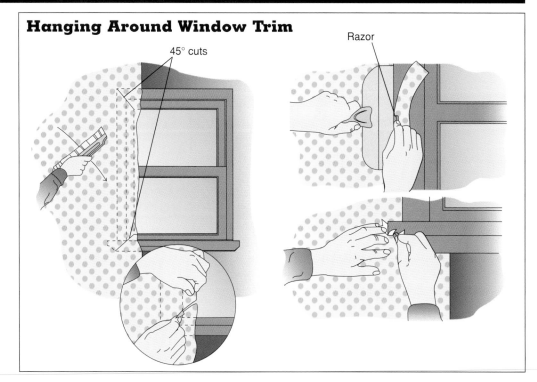

cut away much of the excess at the top half of the opening to get it out of your way. Then cut into the top corner at a 45-degree angle to relieve tension.

3. Drop the bottom half of the covering and repeat steps 1 and 2. For a window, trim away the remaining excess over the window and cut into the bottom corner at a 45-degree angle. For a door, cut away the excess down to the floor.

4. Use the broad knife to push the covering firmly around the trim molding of the opening. Then, using the broad knife as a guide, trim away the excess covering with a razor knife or a razor blade. Finish as usual.

Hanging Around Recessed Windows and Doors

Hang the drop as you would any straight drop, letting it overlap the window or door

You're very lucky if your wallcovering project involves nothing but straight drops. Most installations, like this one, involve corners, split drops, wood trim, cabinets, soffits, electrical cover plates, and similar challenges.

84

Hanging Around Recessed Windows

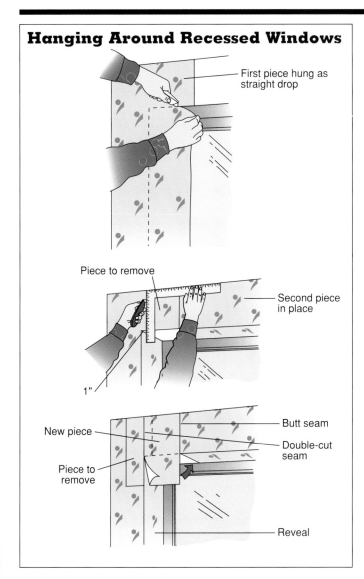

First piece hung as straight drop

Piece to remove

Second piece in place

1"

New piece

Piece to remove

Butt seam

Double-cut seam

Reveal

Wrapping Arches

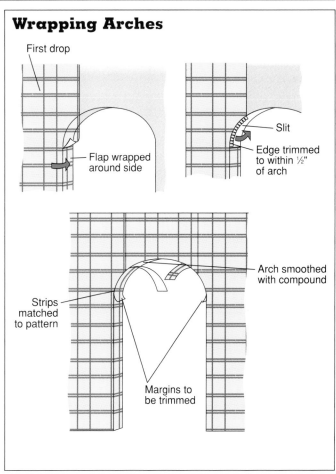

First drop

Flap wrapped around side

Slit

Edge trimmed to within ½" of arch

Strips matched to pattern

Arch smoothed with compound

Margins to be trimmed

---

opening. Smooth the covering right to the edges of the opening. For a window, follow the directions below; for a doorway, skip step 2.

1. At the top, hold the excess material taut with one hand while you make a sliding cut along the edge of the soffit, or header, to the corner.

2. Work the covering around the sill with the broad knife and trim with the razor knife.

3. These cuts release the material for the side flap, which covers the reveal, wrapping around the corner to the win-

dow. Smooth it into place with your brush or broad knife. Cut away any excess material. If it doesn't reach the window, add a new strip as you would for an outside corner.

4. Hang the next sheet (or sheets, as needed) across the top of the window, matching the pattern. Wrap the bottoms of these drops around the edge onto the underside of the soffit, to the window. Smooth and trim along the window. Hang the next full drop and wrap the second side of the window as you did the first.

5. This leaves you with 2 empty spaces on the underside of the soffit, at the ends. Measure in 1 inch from one corner and, using a carpenter's square as a guide, cut through the wallcovering from the ceiling down to the soffit edge. Remove the strip of wallcovering above the window. Repeat on the other corner. You have created a path for new covering to be wrapped from the ceiling into the recess.

6. To cut a filler piece, butt a short section of wallcovering, with pattern matching, against the sheet hanging near the center of the window. The other edge will overlap the sheet at the corner.

7. Paste the filler piece and press it into place. Holding

the material taut with one hand, make a sliding cut along the side of the opening, to the corner. From that point, using your carpenter's square as a guide, make a double-cut seam (see page 81) from the ceiling down to the same corner.

8. Wrap the flap around the edge and smooth it under the soffit. Trim off the excess at the window. Repeat on the other corner.

Hanging Around Arches

Hang the same as recessed windows, except wrap the sides only to the point where the curve begins. A separate strip will cover the curve.

1. Let the drop hang over the opening. Cut from the outer edge to the wall at a point just below the curve. Wrap the flap around the side and smooth into place with your brush.

2. Trim away the excess material within the curved opening to within ½ inch of the edge of the arch. Make small slits at ½- to 1-inch intervals along the remaining margin, stopping the cuts ⅛ inch shy of the edge. Wrap the tabs into the arch.

3. Hang new strips of covering at the top of the arch and down the other side, trimming, slitting, and wrapping it as you did the first drop.

4. Coat the interior of the arch with a lightweight spackling paste to hide the tabs. When the paste is dry, lightly sand with 120-grit sandpaper. Vacuum the dust. Apply a coat of primer/sealer.

5. Measure the width of the arch (thickness of the wall) at 3 points: the apex, or top; midway down the curve; and at the bottom of the curve. Subtract ⅛ inch from the widest of these 3 measurements. Measure the length of the arc from the apex down to the bottom of the curve (half of the arch). Add 1 inch to this measurement—½ inch for the top margin and ½ inch for the bottom margin. Take a large scrap, match it to the pattern at the top of the side flap, and cut to these measurements. Cut a second strip the same way. Paste and book both strips.

6. Set one strip into place with your hands, matching the pattern at the bottom of the arc and working up to the apex. Center the strip so it is about

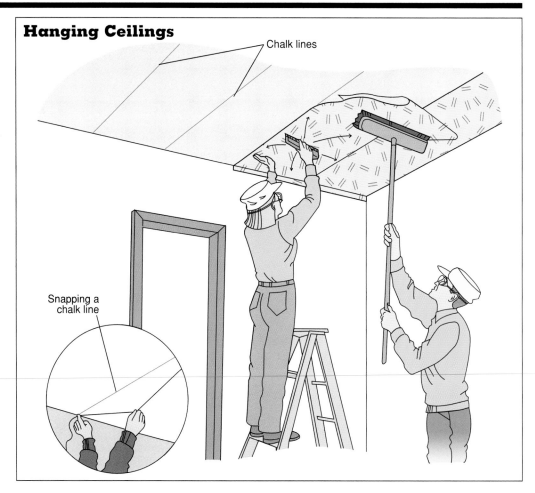

Hanging Ceilings

Chalk lines

Snapping a chalk line

¹⁄₁₆ inch from each edge of the arch. It should overlap both the side flap and the apex centerline by ½ inch. Smooth into place with your brush. Hang the second strip on the other side of the arch.

7. Make a double-cut seam (see page 81) at the apex centerline. Using your broad knife as a guide, cut away the margins at the bottoms of the strips so the strips form butt seams with the side flaps.

Hanging Ceilings

Hang the ceiling before the walls. The location of the first ceiling sheet was determined when you made the layout

(see page 75). Mark the location of the first seam by snapping a chalk line between the 2 marks. Use white or yellow chalk so it won't show through the covering.

Hanging a ceiling always takes 2 people: One holds the covering while the other positions and smoothes it. In other respects the procedure is the same as for walls. Don't forget to allow a 2-inch margin on each end of each strip. Since a wall and ceiling covering can match on only one wall, the match should be at the focal-point wall (assuming it's a long wall).

1. Put the pattern in the correct place at the ceiling line, allowing the margin to over-

lap onto the wall. Place the edge against the chalk line. As you work, keep your hands no more than 2 feet apart.

2. Smooth the sheet into place and push it into the ceiling line with your brush. Repeat this procedure with the remaining sheets. Smooth with the brush and let set 10 to 15 minutes.

3. Finish as for walls. Cut the margins flush with the ceiling line for a ceiling-only installation. Allow the margins to lap onto the wall by ¼ inch for a full-room installation.

4. When you hang the wall, start with the focal-point wall and match the wall pattern to the ceiling pattern. Hang each drop as usual so the 2-inch

Hanging Angled Walls

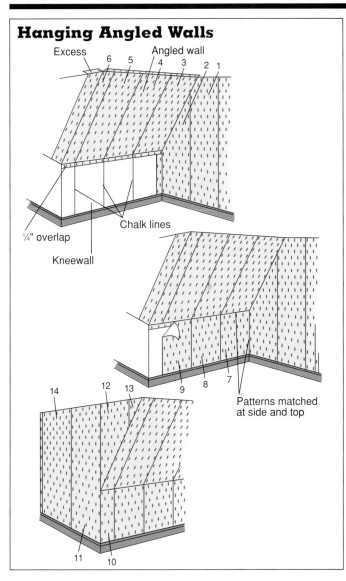

Excess Angled wall

¼" overlap

Chalk lines

Kneewall

Patterns matched
at side and top

Trimming Around Electrical Outlets

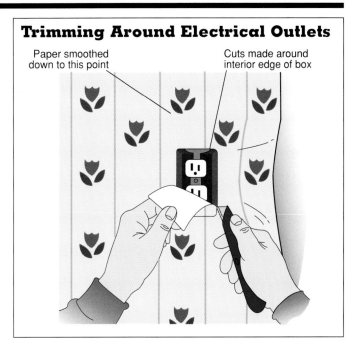

Paper smoothed
down to this point

Cuts made around
interior edge of box

margin overlaps the ceiling.
Score the ceiling line with
your broad knife. Gently peel
the wall sheet back and cut it
along the scored line with scissors or a razor knife. Press the
sheet back into place to make
a lap seam. Finish as usual.
Use vinyl-to-vinyl adhesive if
the covering contains vinyl.

Hanging Angled Walls

Start by covering the wall next
to the angled wall. Let the
inside sheets lap ½ inch onto
the angled wall as for an
inside corner (see page 82).

1. For the first layout lines
on the angled wall and kneewall, measure from the inside
corner a distance equal to the
wallcovering width plus ¼
inch. Snap a chalk line on each
wall at this point. From these
lines measure a distance equal
to the wallcovering's actual
width and repeat the chalk lining. Continue across both walls.

2. Cut all drops with 2-
inch top and bottom margins.
Hang the angle first, making

a lap seam (see page 82) in the
inside corner and wrapping
the outside corner (see page
83). Let the bottom margins
lap onto the kneewall. Finish
as usual, using your broad
knife as a guide and trimming
the bottom margins to ¼ inch.

3. Hang the kneewall next,
matching the pattern at the
top and side seams. Make a
lap seam (see page 82) in the
inside corner and wrap the
outside corner (see page 83).
Let the top margin lap up onto
the angle. As you finish each
sheet, score the line between
the angled wall and the kneewall with a broad knife, then
peel back the top piece and cut
away the excess from the
angled-wall strip with scissors
or a knife. Smooth the kneewall strip back into place with
your brush and roll the seam.

4. Proceed with the first full
sheet on the new wall as described for outside corners,
page 83. Cut a straight piece
(or pieces) to fill in the triangle

created by the angled wall.
Using your broad knife as a
guide, make a double-cut
seam (see page 81) ¼ inch
from the angle's edge.

Hanging Around Obstacles

Installing a wallcovering
around an immovable
obstruction requires some
special techniques.

Trimming Around Electrical Outlets

The cover plates should be
removed from the outlets and
the electricity turned off prior
to hanging the wallcovering.
As with door and window
openings, hang the wallcovering right over the outlet boxes,
cutting out the covering by
making a sliding cut around
the edges of the outlet box.
Avoid deep cuts that could
damage wires.

Covering Electrical Faceplates

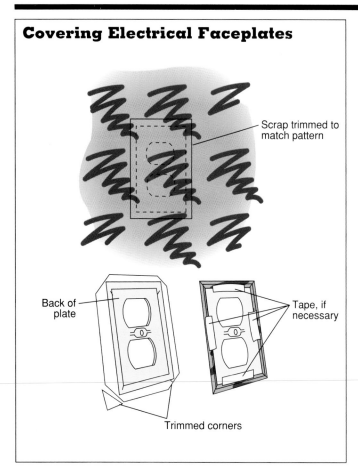

Scrap trimmed to match pattern

Back of plate

Tape, if necessary

Trimmed corners

Hanging Around a Light Fixture

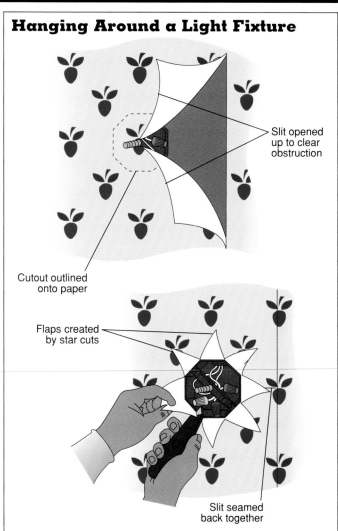

Slit opened up to clear obstruction

Cutout outlined onto paper

Flaps created by star cuts

Slit seamed back together

Covering Electrical Faceplates

Covering switchplates, outlet covers, and other panels with the wallcovering gives a room a professional appearance.

1. Match a scrap of the wallcovering to the area around the opening. Cut the patch 1 inch bigger than the switchplate all around and match it to the pattern again.

2. Sand the face of the plate with 120-grit sandpaper. Coat with the primer/sealer used on the wall. Let dry.

3. Temporarily remount the plate. Position the patch over it, matching the pattern to the surrounding wall. With a #1 pencil lightly mark the corners of the plate and the screw

holes. Remove the wallcovering and plate from the wall.

4. Apply vinyl-to-vinyl paste to the face of the plate and the backside of the covering. Place the covering over the plate, matching the corner marks and screw holes. Place face down on a table. Trim the margins to within ½ inch of the plate's edge. Trim the corners at 45-degree angles and wrap the edges onto the back of the plate. Set aside to dry. Secure the back edges with masking tape, if necessary.

5. After the paste dries, carefully cut out the receptacle holes with a razor knife. Then remount the switchplate. Wash and towel-dry the plate and the surrounding wall.

Hanging Around Light Fixtures

If you were able to remove the entire fixture and mounting canopy when you prepped the room, only the electrical box remains in place. The electricity should be off. Hang the covering over the fixture as over an electrical outlet box. If the fixture or a protruding bracket remains, you will have to cut slits into the wallcovering. First slit the covering from the nearest edge so it will slide around the center screw. Work the covering into place around the box. Then lightly mark the perime-

ter of the box on the covering. Make star cuts (see above) at 1-inch intervals from the center out to the perimeter of the box. Trim away the excess, smooth the remaining covering around the box edge, and seam the slit back together. Finish as usual.

Hanging Around Radiators

For radiators, slip the wallcovering behind the radiator and, if you can't reach your brush behind it, use a yardstick or radiator brush to press the covering into place. Do not let the covering hang loose.

HANGING DECORATIVE BORDERS

Borders do wonders for a room, but their prominence requires that you hang them with care. The basics for hanging a border are the same whether it goes at the ceiling line, which is called a frieze, at chair-rail height, or around windows and doors. A border placed at chair-rail height is called a dado when there is no chair-rail molding.

Planning the Layout

Most borders come in 5-yard rolls. Plan your lengths accordingly, allowing for the ½ inch of material lost when you cut inside corners, the same as a wallcovering (see page 82). Frieze, dado, and chair-rail borders start in the dead corner. Before you hang the border, check the material for flaws and back-roll it, the same as a wallcovering (see page 71). Then, as follows, snap horizontal guidelines to mark the border's location on the wall.

Frieze (Ceiling-Line) Borders

Measure the width of the border. Measure this distance down from the ceiling and mark it at each end of the wall. Snap a chalk line between the marks. The border's bottom edge will align with this line. Repeat on all the room's walls.

Dado Borders

Typically, the bottom edge of a border would be 32 to 33 inches above the floor, the traditional chair-rail height. However, if your border is wide, center it on a line 33 inches above the floor, to maintain attractive proportions in the room. Other heights are acceptable, especially if they align with architectural features such as windowsills, or if they border chair-rail moldings. Decide how high you want the border before proceeding.

Then measure the distance from the floor to the height at which you want the bottom edge of the border. Subtract

Frieze borders like this one are installed along the ceiling line after the wallcoverings are hung.

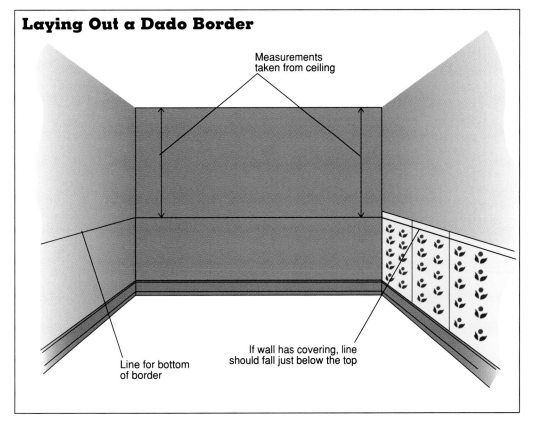

Laying Out a Dado Border

Measurements taken from ceiling

Line for bottom of border

If wall has covering, line should fall just below the top

this measurement from the room's height. Then measure this distance down from the ceiling and mark it at both ends of the wall. Snap a chalk line between the marks. The border's bottom edge will align with this line.

Door, Window, and Chair-Rail Borders

The trim moldings give you a physical edge against which to place the covering.

Preparing the Wall

Prepare the border area with a primer/sealer, the same as for a wallcovering (see page 75). Use the chalk lines as guides.

Pasting and Booking Borders

Cut the border to the proper lengths for each wall, joining them anywhere the ends meet on a given wall. Most border patterns match end to end and you join them with a butt seam. If your pattern doesn't match end to end, join the pieces with a double-cut seam (see page 81).

Review the instructions for prepasted and unpasted coverings (pages 76 to 79), whichever applies to your border. You will handle the border the same way, with two exceptions:

1. Book each strip in an accordion fold, paste to paste and pattern to pattern, and let it sit for 3 to 5 minutes. This will make the border easier to handle when hanging.

2. After a prepasted border has rested 3 to 5 minutes, open it and coat it with a vinyl-to-vinyl paste so you get the best possible adhesion. Paste and book 2 lengths at a time.

Hanging Borders

Ideally, 2 people work together to hang a border. One feeds the border to the other, who smooths it into place. Hang from left to right if you are right-handed, right to left if you are left-handed, unfolding 2-foot segments at a time. With one exception, you will hang the border just like a wallcovering, including cutting inside corners and wrapping outside corners. The one exception is mitering the corners around doors and windows.

Frieze (Ceiling-Line) and Dado Borders

Start in the dead corner. Unfold 2 feet of border, align its bottom edge with the guideline, and smooth into place with your hands. Brush to ensure a firm seal. At the end of a roll, join to the next roll with a butt seam or a double-cut seam (see page 81) as appropriate and continue around the room.

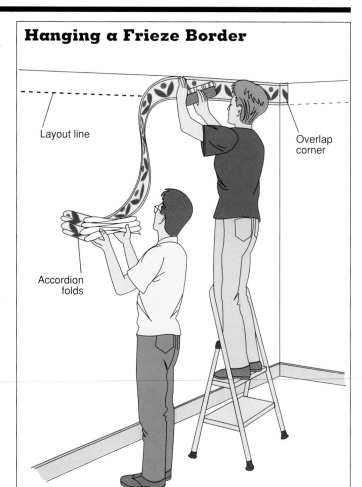

Hanging a Frieze Border

Layout line

Accordion folds

Overlap corner

Dado Border With Wallcovering Below or Above

Review the hanging techniques for half-wall wallcoverings on page 82 before you begin.

Wallcovering Below

You already snapped a new guideline on top of this base covering (see page 82). Starting in the dead corner, set the border's bottom edge on this line. Using a carpenter's square as a guide, make a double-cut seam (see page 81) along the border's bottom edge. Work carefully so you don't cut the border. Lift the border, remove the excess base covering, and smooth the border back into place.

Wallcovering Above

You already snapped a new guideline on top of this upper covering (see page 82). Starting in the dead corner, set the border's top edge directly on this line. Using your carpenter's square as a guide, make a double-cut seam (see page 81) along the border's top edge. Work carefully so you don't cut the border and no seam shows. Lift the border, remove the excess base covering, and smooth the border back into place.

Hanging a Dado With Wallcovering Below

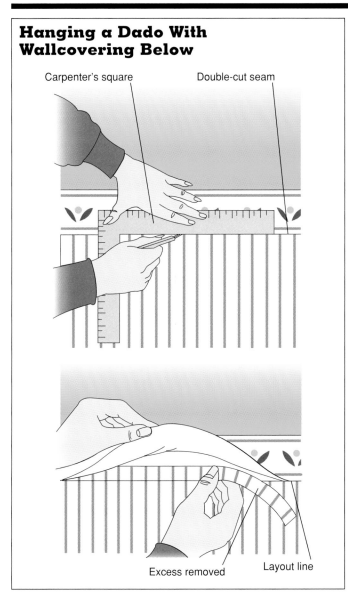

Carpenter's square

Double-cut seam

Excess removed

Layout line

Hanging a Dado With Two Coverings

½ width of border

Seam

Line for bottom of border

Mitering Border Corners

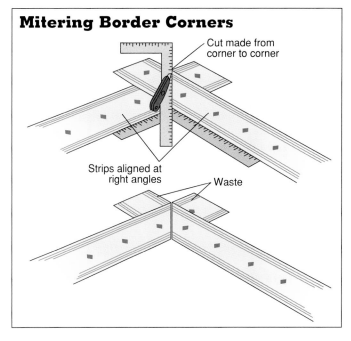

Cut made from corner to corner

Strips aligned at right angles

Waste

Dado Border With Wallcovering Above and Below

Review the technique for hanging 2 coverings on a wall (page 82). A border should be centered over the seam line where the 2 coverings join. Measure the width of the border. Measure half this dimension down from the seam line and snap a guideline. Paste and book the border (use vinyl-to-vinyl paste if the materials contain vinyl). Starting in the dead corner, set the border's bottom edge directly on the guideline. Gently lift up the border's bottom edge, wipe away the guideline, and smooth the border back into place.

Mitering Right-Angle Corners

Some border applications, such as those around a window, create right-angle corners. These look best if they are mitered, or cut on the diagonal. Cut the lengths so they will extend several inches beyond one another when they meet. Lay them on your worktable exactly as they will meet on the wall, top and bottom strips over side pieces. Use your carpenter's square to make sure they join at a true 90-degree angle. Using the square as a guide, make a diagonal double-cut seam between the outside and inside corners of the angle. Hang the 2 strips the same as other borders.

F INISHING UP

When you finish hanging the last sheet, step back and give your work a careful inspection. No matter how good a job you have done, there are bound to be some small flaws. The most common are bubbles, creases, loose edges, and small tears. Let your covering dry, then follow these instructions to eliminate them.

Correcting Imperfections

If, try as you will, you can't match the pattern, do not force the paper. This only overstretches it, causing its seams to pull apart as it dries. Instead, if the mismatch occurs with the top half of the sheet, pull it completely off the wall and start over. If it occurs on the bottom half, pull it away from the wall up to the midsection and reset. If this doesn't work, pull the entire sheet off the wall and hang a new sheet. Use the same approach if the wallcovering won't lie flat.

Bubbles and wrinkles present a different problem. First, distinguish between the two. Bubbles are raised spots in the covering. Wrinkles are creases. Don't be overly concerned with either one. Most disappear as your wallcovering dries, so be patient. However, if these defects remain after the covering is dry, you can repair them.

You need a paste syringe and two products in addition to your application tools to do this job. One product is a paste, either vinyl-to-vinyl adhesive or seam-and-border adhesive, thinned 50:50 with water. The other is a saturating solution made of equal parts hot water and white vinegar. Complete each repair by wiping the area clean with a damp sponge and toweling it dry.

Bubbles

First, do you have a hard bubble or an air pocket? Gently press the spot. You feel nothing behind an air pocket. You feel a slight ridge or ring behind a hard bubble.

Eliminating Air Pockets

Air pockets occur when air gets trapped behind the paper. Use one of two methods to eliminate them.

To fix a small bubble, puncture the bottom edge of the bubble with the paste syringe. This lets out the air. Puncture big bubbles twice, once at the top edge and once at the bottom edge. Shoot the thinned paste up into the air space. Use just enough to get it wet. Let stand 3 to 5 minutes. Carefully press the wallcovering back onto the wall. Brush from the perimeter into the center. Clean up any excess paste.

To fix a large bubble, measure out ½ inch on each side at the top of the bubble. Lightly mark these points with a pencil. Make a similar mark ½

inch below the center of the bubble's bottom edge. Make a V cut connecting these 3 points with your wallpaper knife. For busy patterns, you can slit the bubble with an X. Wet the defective area with the saturating solution. Carefully lift up the flap when the covering has softened. Gently clean out the space under it. Be careful not to delaminate the covering or damage its edges. Spread a thin coat of adhesive on the wall and the backside of the flap. Let it sit 2 to 3 minutes or until just about dry. Starting at the top, gently brush down with your smoothing brush until the flap adheres to the wall. Then gently roll up and then back

down with your seam roller. Clean up the excess paste.

Removing Hard Bubbles

Hard bubbles occur when you overpaste a wallcovering. Remove paste lumps with one of these two methods.

Method 1 involves taking a big scrap of the wallcovering and matching the pattern. From it cut a piece 3 inches larger than the bubble in each direction. Test it again for pattern match. Activate this piece by wetting or pasting as appropriate. Book by folding over. Place in a plastic bag and let rest for 3 to 5 minutes. Meanwhile, open the damaged area by cutting as close as possible around the lump. Do not cut the wallboard behind it. Spray the spot with

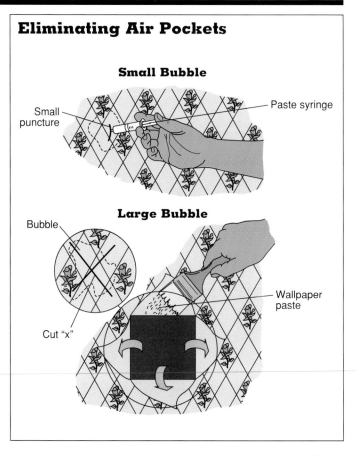

Eliminating Air Pockets

Small Bubble

Small puncture

Paste syringe

Large Bubble

Bubble

Cut "x"

Wallpaper paste

the saturating solution. When it is softened, peel off the wallcovering, scrape out the lump, and clean the surface behind it. Let dry thoroughly. Lay the pasted piece over the hole. Match the pattern on all 4 sides. Then, carefully cutting through both layers, make curved cuts above and below the bubble, creating a football-shaped patch. Put this patch into the plastic bag. Rewet the area with the saturating solution. When the edges loosen, pull off the wallcovering remaining inside the curved cuts. Press the patch into place, smoothing it with the brush. Roll the edges lightly with your seam roller. Clean the patch area.

To use Method 2, make a *V* cut and repaste as described on opposite page, eliminating air pockets.

Wrinkles

Wrinkles come from overstretching the covering. First, do you have a hollow wrinkle or a hard wrinkle? A hollow wrinkle looks like a minor fold in the covering. A hard wrinkle looks like a sharp crease in the covering. Take one of two corrective steps.

Smoothing Out Hollow Wrinkles

Use either of the methods outlined on opposite page for removing air pockets. If you use a *V* cut, do not seal the flap with a seam roller. Instead, brush upward over the repair with your smoothing brush.

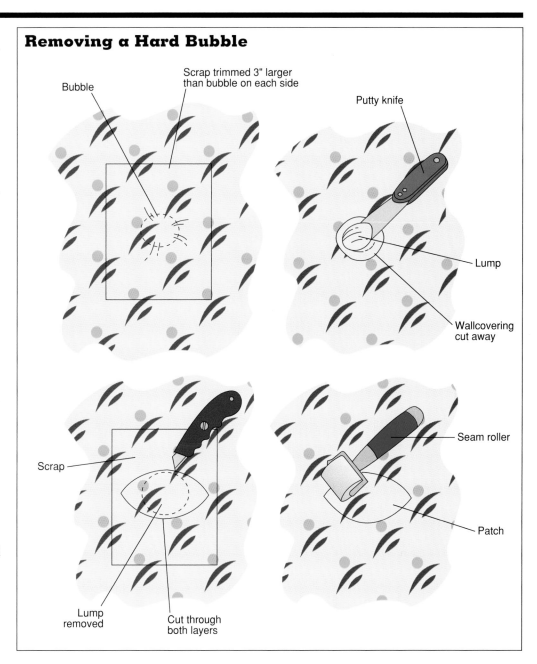

Removing a Hard Bubble

Bubble

Scrap trimmed 3" larger than bubble on each side

Putty knife

Lump

Wallcovering cut away

Scrap

Lump removed

Cut through both layers

Seam roller

Patch

Eliminating Hard Wrinkles

Preheat an iron at the polyester or permanent-press setting. Hold a wet terry washcloth over the crease and press the hot iron over the spot. Check the wrinkle every 30 seconds until it has softened but not pulled away from the wall. Roll the wrinkle with your seam roller, working to smooth the crease. If this does not work, repeat the process until the wrinkle disappears. If, after several tries, the wrinkle is still evident, use Method 1 for removing hard bubbles (see opposite page).

Cleaning Up

Discard leftover paste. There's no point in saving it because it quickly loses its grip. Save large scraps and partially used bolts for future repairs. Reroll them in their original direction and secure with #14 rubber bands. Place in a large plastic bag; tie; and store in a dark, dry place such as an attic.

When Wallcovering Needs Repairs

The keys to long life for your wallcovering are to use the correct wallcovering for the room and to hang it properly. Promptly repair any damage.

Repasting Seams

Loose seams are easy to repair. First, soften the seam with a 50:50 solution of hot water and white vinegar. Thin a vinyl-to-vinyl or seam-and-border adhesive 50:50 with water. Pull away the covering and apply thinned paste under it. Smooth into place with your hands and then gently roll the seam, working up. Clean the area with a damp sponge and towel-dry.

If a lifting seam occurs in a high-moisture area, check for mold and mildew. If you find them, peel back the covering and wash and sterilize behind it (see page 33 for instructions). Let dry thoroughly. Then reseal with seam-and-border or vinyl-to-vinyl adhesive.

Repairing a Tear

1. Carefully match a large scrap of the wallcovering to the pattern on the wall. Tack it into place with masking tape.

2. Using your carpenter's square, cut through both layers, making the patch 6 inches bigger than the tear on each side. Remove the masking tape and patch.

3. Apply paste to the scrap and book it by folding it over. Let it sit until it gets tacky.

Soften the damaged area with a solution of equal parts hot water and white vinegar. Lift out the old covering.

4. Put the pasted patch in position, matching the pattern. Smooth it with your brush. Roll the seams. Clean the area with a sponge and clear water. Towel-dry.

Cleaning Wallcoverings

If you can, dust all wallcoverings weekly to prevent dirt buildup. Most stains come out with any degreaser or spray-foam carpet and upholstery cleaner sold for home use. Test any cleaning product in an inconspicuous spot.

•Washable wallcoverings: Clean occasionally with a mild detergent and cold water applied with soft cloth or sponge. Treat stains before you wash the entire surface.

•Scrubbable wallcoverings: Scrub as often as necessary with a brush and a mild detergent and warm water.

•Nonwashable wallcoverings: Blot the affected area with a sponge moistened with mild detergent and cold water. Don't scrub. Blot again with cold water and dry. For stubborn stains, ask your wallcovering dealer to recommend a spot remover. For overall griminess, use a commercial wallpaper dough (it won't remove stains). Ask your dealer about sprays to make new nonvinyl wallcovering stain and dirt resistant.

U.S./Metric Measure Conversion Chart

		Formulas for Exact Measures			**Rounded Measures for Quick Reference**		
	Symbol	When you know:	Multiply by:	To find:			
Mass	oz	ounces	28.35	grams	1 oz		= 30 g
(weight)	lb	pounds	0.45	kilograms	4 oz		= 115 g
	g	grams	0.035	ounces	8 oz		= 225 g
	kg	kilograms	2.2	pounds	16 oz	= 1 lb	= 450 g
					32 oz	= 2 lb	= 900 g
					36 oz	= 2¼ lb	= 1000 g (1 kg)
Volume	pt	pints	0.47	liters	1 c	= 8 oz	= 250 ml
	qt	quarts	0.95	liters	2 c (1 pt)	= 16 oz	= 500 ml
	gal	gallons	3.785	liters	4 c (1 qt)	= 32 oz	= 1 liter
	ml	milliliters	0.034	fluid ounces	4 qt (1 gal)	= 128 oz	= 3¾ liter
Length	in.	inches	2.54	centimeters	⅜ in.	= 1 cm	
	ft	feet	30.48	centimeters	1 in.	= 2.5 cm	
	yd	yards	0.9144	meters	2 in.	= 5 cm	
	mi	miles	1.609	kilometers	2½ in.	= 6.5 cm	
	km	kilometers	0.621	miles	12 in. (1 ft)	= 30 cm	
	m	meters	1.094	yards	1 yd	= 90 cm	
	cm	centimeters	0.39	inches	100 ft	= 30 m	
					1 mi	= 1.6 km	
Temperature	° F	Fahrenheit	⅝ (after subtracting 32)	Celsius	32° F	= 0° C	
	° C	Celsius	⅞ (then add 32)	Fahrenheit	68° F	= 20° C	
					212° F	= 100° C	
Area	in.²	square inches	6.452	square centimeters	1 in.²	= 6.5 cm²	
	ft²	square feet	929.0	square centimeters	1 ft²	= 930 cm²	
	yd²	square yards	8361.0	square centimeters	1 yd²	= 8360 cm²	
	a.	acres	0.4047	hectares	1 a.	= 4050 m²	

INDEX